W9-DGC-916

By the same author

Balm in Gilead and Other Plays
The Rimers of Eldritch and Other Plays
The Gingham Dog
Lemon Sky
The Hot l Baltimore
The Mound Builders

5th of July

A play by Lanford Wilson

5th of July

A Mermaid Dramabook

HILL AND WANG   NEW YORK

A DIVISION OF FARRAR STRAUS GIROUX

© 1978 by Lanford Wilson

All rights reserved

Published simultaneously in Canada

by McGraw-Hill Ryerson Ltd., Toronto

Printed in the United States of America

Designed by Karen Watt

Photographs from the original production by Ken Howard

First Hill & Wang edition, 1979

Library of Congress Cataloging in Publication Data
Wilson, Lanford
5th of July.
(A Mermaid dramabook)
I. Title.
PS3573.I458F5   1979   812'.5'4   78–26477
ISBN 0–8090–4455–2
ISBN 0–8090–1240–5 pbk.

Eighth printing, 1986

For Frank Anderson

5th of July was first presented by the Circle Repertory Company, in New York City, on April 27, 1978. It was directed by Marshall W. Mason; the setting was by John Lee Beatty; costumes were by Laura Crow; lighting was by Marc B. Weiss; the original song was by Jonathan Hogan; sound was by Chuck London; and the production stage manager was Fred Reinglas. The cast, in order of appearance, was as follows:

KENNETH TALLEY, JR. / William Hurt
JOHN LANDIS / Jonathan Hogan
GWEN LANDIS / Nancy Snyder
JED JENKINS / Jeff Daniels
JUNE TALLEY / Joyce Reehling
SHIRLEY TALLEY / Amy Wright
SALLY FRIEDMAN / Helen Stenborg
WESTON HURLEY / Danton Stone

5th of July ran at the Circle Repertory for a total of 168 performances. Timothy Shelton replaced William Hurt in the role of Ken Talley, Jr., for the last sixteen weeks.

5th of July

CHARACTERS

KENNETH TALLEY, JR., had both legs shot off seven years ago in the Vietnam War. He is thirty-five, strong, good-looking, and a touch cynical, but not deeply.

JED JENKINS, his lover, twenty-five. Larger, stronger, and an almost silent listener.

JUNE TALLEY, Ken's sister, thirty-three.

SHIRLEY TALLEY, her daughter, fourteen.

JOHN LANDIS, childhood friend of the Talleys, thirty-five. Deeply cynical.

GWEN LANDIS, his wife, thirty-three. Racy.

WESTON HURLEY, composer friend of Gwen and John's, twenty-five. Listens late.

SALLY FRIEDMAN, Ken and June's aunt, sixty-seven. Not really batty; preoccupied.

TIME

Act I: Early evening, Independence Day, 1977

Act II: The following morning

PLACE

The Talley place, a farm near Lebanon, Missouri

The set is the large sun porch/family room of a prosperous southern Missouri farmhouse built around 1860.

We see the wide doors to a hallway upstage, and a stairway going up. At one side doors open to a porch that wraps around most or all of the house. In Act II this porch, with the living room in the background, will be facing the audience.

The room is furnished with a large sofa, two matching armchairs, tables, a desk, bookshelves filled with books on plants, language, literature, etc.

KEN *sits at a desk. He is very hung over, and in this state tends to be blandly cynical.*

He is listening to a small portable tape recorder. The recording is of a boy who speaks with great hesitation, mangling words so badly nothing is intelligible to us. KEN *listens, makes notes, rubs his eyes and head.*

JOHN *enters, dropping his hat, a camera, and a shopping bag where they fall.*

JOHN: Hey, teacher. I don't believe you're still listening to that same damn thing.

KEN: (*Turning the recording off mid-line*) This kid's too shy to talk to me so I gave him a cassette and he's telling this very strange science-fiction story about—

JOHN: (*Conspiring*) Listen, you can't push her, and I'm not promising anything, but she's crazy about Lebanon, she loves your house. She might decide to take it. It looks good.

KEN: Oh, God, John, that would be great. I know it needs work, but—

JOHN: Would you look at you. You look like shit. We had a party last night, didn't we. Goddamn, it's good to see you. We gotta take some time together. Just the two of us, you know?

KEN: Did you get the message? I left it outside your door, I beat on—

JOHN: Oh, yeah. Suzy Mitchell.

KEN: She said it was a matter of life and death.

JOHN: Who is she?

KEN: (*Pause*) I beat on your door; I woke everyone in the house except you two.

JOHN: Oh, shit. I'm sorry. We go to sleep, we die.

KEN: I remember. And an Arthur Schwartzkoff called around noon and said to return—

JOHN: How did they get this number? (*Picking up phone*) We didn't tell anybody we were stopping over here.

KEN: And a plasterer called and wanted to know if—

JOHN: Baby, just don't pick up; don't mess with it. It's never worth it.

KEN: Two years ago you and Gwen came by St. Louis for dinner, we've been getting calls ever since.

JOHN: Hey, how about that new high school building? That's what we were campaigning for, remember? Ten years ago.

KEN: Fifteen, but who's counting.

JOHN: (*On phone*) Honey, this is a credit-card call, card number 072-6913-037L. L . . . as in Love your Lovely voice. Thank *you*.

KEN: The old one collapsed.

JOHN: You're shittin' me. It finally fell in?

KEN: Unfortunately nobody was in—

JOHN: (*On phone*) Yeah, this is Jack, he in? Goddamn, we are really missing each other today. Have him call, but person-to-person.

KEN: Did you give a plasterer this number?

JOHN: (*Hanging up*) Boy, I don't know. A real plasterer?

KEN: He wanted to know if you intended the studio completely blocked off from the dining room.

JOHN: Where?

KEN: I told him to go ahead.

JOHN: Which house?

GWEN: (*Offstage, yelling*) Honey, did you call that prick in Nashville?

JOHN: Negative. We're takin' dinner with him tomorrow at eight.

KEN: Here?

JOHN: No, there. (*To* GWEN) He's in the bag.

GWEN: (*Entering*) How come I never knew you were born in a mansion? Creep.

KEN: Yeah. John said you liked it. That's great.

GWEN: I'm crazy about your town, it's a fuckin' hoot. I'm mad about the house. It's only *Christina's World,* you realize that. I've never been so at peace in my life. What's the ribbons? (*She is all over the house, collecting tapes*)

KEN: What ribbons?

JOHN: All down to the river.

GWEN: (*Overlapping*) Those red ribbons tied to sticks all down the hill.

KEN: That's where Jed has planted his—whatever it is—hedges. In only five years you'll be able to see the plants.

GWEN: (*To* JOHN) Yeah, he says he's going to make a fucking English garden.

KEN: He baby-sat the cuttings all winter. Turned this sun porch into a greenhouse. All the floors were covered with buckets of sticks, rooting. Makes you understand why they call it a nursery.

GWEN: Does he talk to them? Or is that just a lot of bull?

JOHN: Must talk to something.

GWEN: You were here all winter?

KEN: He was here all winter. I certainly was not.

GWEN: What kind of lover sits down here alone all winter, rooting hedges?

KEN: A botanical lover.

JOHN: Broke your heart, right? Don't forget we know you.

KEN: He came up to St. Louis a couple of times. I came down here. Once.

GWEN: How is it in the winter here?

KEN: Very austere.

JOHN: You got heat?

GWEN: I'm gonna love it. (*Exits upstairs*)

KEN: Oh, yes. I put in a new furnace. (*To* JOHN) Listen, can we talk about this before Jed . . . gets back up here.

GWEN: (*Returns*) You seen our bathing suits? June said they were drying. I can't find the dryer.

KEN: There isn't a dryer.

JED: (*Comes up on the porch*) Light's going. Can't see a thing down there.

KEN: You couldn't hide in the garden all night.

GWEN: (*Opens the door. To* JED) Hey, come in. We're dishing you to filth.

JOHN: Honey, we gotta get dressed if we're going to this shindig.

KEN: It's hardly a shindig. You don't—

GWEN: Listen, I got nothing but love and respect for Matt Friedman. I mean, he really straightened me out. Like he wouldn't let me sell my houses or anything and he wouldn't let me take flying lessons. I mean, he was like a leveling influence. He said I had a grave responsibility.

KEN: He didn't mean his, however.

GWEN: He was really pissed because Schwartzkoff appointed his wife's nephew to handle the trust. And if that isn't nepotism, like by definition, I don't know what is.

KEN: Oh, did I give you that message?

JOHN: (*To* GWEN) C'mon, 's go.

GWEN: Would you look at that fucking sunset!

KEN: Guaranteed every night.

JOHN: (*To* KEN) You going to be all right? Can you get down to the river okay?

KEN: (*Overlapping*) We're not going cross-country. We'll take the car. It's all madly illegal anyway. There's no reason for you two to come. There's no ceremony.

JOHN: No, Gwen's got a real bug up her ass.

GWEN: (*They are leaving*) No shit, like I feel a responsibility, you know?

KEN: There's no reason— (*They are gone*)

GWEN: (*Offstage. Singing country-Western*) Rock of ages, cleft for me. Let me hide— (*She's been goosed*) Don't, no, don't— stop! (*She giggles. The door slams. The moment they leave,* SHIRLEY *comes out of hiding and follows them to the door, grandly ignoring* KEN. KEN *stares at her blandly. After the door slams, she again snubs* KEN *and hurries off after* JOHN *and* GWEN)

JED: (*Comes into the room. A pause. He is putting his watch on*) They're only going to be here—another twenty-one hours. I can hang in there if you can. (*He goes to the planter table*) You look like you're in real great shape.

KEN: Oh, I'm fine. On a scale of one to ten I'm about to show up on the chart any minute now. How could I ever have had the energy to live with those two.

JED: And June.

KEN: She moved out. You cannot believe how little you missed by going to bed last night.

JED: That was the point.

KEN: You made that clear.

JED: I tried.

KEN: Reminiscences, and camaraderie, and everyone had an awful lot of medicine. Snow rained like . . . snow.

JED: Everything's going crazy down there. The lavender's all over the thyme, the angelica's flopping all over the germander—

KEN: (*As* JED *kisses him*) Holy Christ, you smell terrific!

JED: Come on, under that fragrance I'm rank as a goat. He was down there telling me about their garden in Carmel, I was really pissed. I was throwing that lavender over my back, the whole garden smells like an English bathhouse. Check it out early, it'll be grown over again by noon.

KEN: What'd you think of him in the strong light of day?

JED: He looks fine. A little sneaky.

KEN: Yeah, well . . . I think, given my choice between them now, I'd take her.

JED: Given my choice, I'd take hemlock.

KEN: He took her all over town. We haven't talked money, but she's crazy about the town, she's crazy about the land, she's crazy about the house.

JED: What does that tell you?

KEN: Exactly. The question is, is she crazy enough to buy it. I've seen her become remarkably lucid with a checkbook in her hand.

JUNE: (*Entering*) Are we going—oh, fine, you look like hell. Take care of yourself, for God's sake. Are we doing this?

KEN: There's no hurry. They went in to change. I suppose into something black.

JUNE: You told them it wasn't formal?

KEN: I wouldn't presume.

JUNE: Where's Aunt Sally? Is she ready?

KEN: Maybe not ready and willing, but probably able.

JUNE: (*Going out to the porch*) I really love being the villain in this; I'm really crazy about that. (*Offstage*) Shirley! (SHIR-LEY *appears from downstairs, and runs out*)

KEN: (*Alone with* JED) I'm going to bite that toe.

JED: What toe?

KEN: That toe. That toe. The big dirty one.

JED: (*Tucks foot under him*) I thought snow was heroin.

KEN: For all I know, by now it is. But when we were very young, we were very merry, we rode back and forth all night on the Sausalito ferry, snorting snow. Snow was cocaine, and very dear, even then.

JED: What does that matter to her. She probably owns Peru, or wherever it comes from.

KEN: She does not own Peru. She owns Montana and Colorado. Colorado owns Peru. Oh, God, all the old Berkeley days came back to wreck us last night. We called each other "man" and "cat," you would have vomited. I'll bet I said "dig it" five hundred times. It's a damned wonder we weren't down in the garden singing "We Shall Overcome." We wake you?

JED: Not me.

KEN: Even you. Even the dead. The little people in the wood. I didn't get to bed till five-thirty. All the birds were having fits: "Get the fuck off that goddamned nest, get down in that garden and get me a bug!" Got up at ten . . . that's six-thirty, seven-thirty . . . (*Counting on his fingers*)

JED: Four and a half. Did you eat?

KEN: I had coffee. I didn't even recognize it.

JED: You take your pills?

KEN: After last night my system would go into shock if I sent down one more chemical or another— (JED *starts to get up.* SALLY *enters from upstairs, carrying a macrame basket and a dried rose*) Yes, yes, I took my vitamins, I took my minerals, and my protein and my birth-control pill. Now, if I only had something to start it all moving. I've been up almost twelve hours, my heart hasn't beaten more than five times.

SALLY: (*She is looking for something*) All right, you wretch. I know you're in here somewhere. This is fair warning.

KEN: Nothing has run through here in the last—

SALLY: You haven't seen a roll of copper wire? The beast is being very difficult this evening. (*Hands the rose to* KEN) What does that feel like? Is that dry? I think that's perfectly dry.

KEN: Yes, that is perfectly dry and perfectly hideous-looking.

SALLY: The magazine said it would retain its color . . .

KEN: What color was it? (WESTON *enters, strumming his guitar*)

SALLY: (*To* KEN) Have you seen a—

KEN: Darling, don't start anything now. We'll be leaving any minute.

SALLY: (*At sofa, finds scissors*) There you are. How did you get down there? Lurking down between the cushions, waiting to jab someone in the fanny. (*She sees* WESTON) You're Wes Hurley, aren't you?

JED: Gwen's composer friend.

KEN: You met him last night, darling.

SALLY: I remember last night perfectly.

JUNE: (*Entering, to* WESTON) Are they changing? (WESTON *stares at each in turn*) Gwen and John. Are they changing?

KEN: Are they changing?

WESTON: How . . . do you mean . . . changing?

KEN: Clothes.

WESTON: Oh, wow, I had this whole metamorphosis thing going . . . I was reading this book about Kafka . . .

KEN: (*Overlapping*) They want to come with us tonight, so we are presumably waiting on them.

WESTON: I don't know. They shut the door. (*He goes out to the porch*)

KEN: That means that they're going at it. Every day in every way I'm getting stronger and stronger.

SALLY: How long are you all staying, Wes?

JED: Twenty-one hours.

SALLY: What kind of a visit is that?

KEN: We're lucky they managed to stop by to look at the house at all.

SALLY: Oh, they aren't serious about this house. You're just going to have to stay down here and teach like you're supposed to.

KEN: (*Overlapping*) Under no circumstances will I teach, and they are very serious about it, and you are not to say anything that will gum it up.

SALLY: Gwen doesn't want this house. She could buy any house in the country.

JED: Oh, let him fantasize.

KEN: Darling, please do keep those thoughts to yourself for this weekend.

SALLY: Well, what does she want with a barn like this?

KEN: I had to mention it, right?

JUNE: They want their own recording studio. Away from Nashville.

KEN: And God knows this place is away from almost anything you could think of.

SALLY: The place would be up for sale again in a year.

KEN: You know that, and I know that, but we're getting a little desperate. If Gwen hadn't shown up, I was ready to give it to the Catholics.

SALLY: Wouldn't that be a scandal. You'd be tarred.

KEN: And feathered. I love it. As long as we get a hundred seventy-five for it, I don't care what they do with it.

JED: What did you pay for the house in wherever it is?

SALLY: Oh, I can't think about it.

JUNE: Ninety-five.

SALLY: I don't know why I let your father talk me into moving to California. Matt and I always hated the idea of retirement communities. Imagine choosing to live in the only place in the country that has a full one hundred percent unemployment.

JUNE: Mom and Dad love it.

SALLY: Well, I'm sorry. Retirement shouldn't be squandered on old people. It's morbid. The community planners have made everything so safe and so perfect and peaceful, you are just continually aware of the catch. All the women in their ballet classes and craft classes, getting tangled up in their macrame. Even your mother. Did you get a basket from your mother for Christmas?

KEN: Ummm.

SALLY: Yes, so did I. That sort of thing should really be left to the Indians. And I don't like the house.

KEN: You've hardly seen the house.

SALLY: No, it's too . . . big.

JUNE: Why are you buying it?

SALLY: Well, Buddy swears I'm lonely now that Matt's gone. Really, he's only afraid of who might move in next to him. But I don't love St. Louis any more, no one does.

JUNE: There's nothing wrong with St. Louis.

JED: There's nothing right about it.

SALLY: The mayor on TV looks like he'd rather be the mayor of any other place on earth. And you aren't going to get anywhere with Shirley while I'm around.

JUNE: (*Overlapping*) Don't let that worry you.

SALLY: (*Spots spool of something*) Is that you? No, you're the green tape. I'll need you, too. How can people ever organize a hobby? It's just exhausting. Is it going to rain? I suppose they'll cancel the dance and the fireworks. Probably they'll move it to the Community Hall.

KEN: A fireworks display in the Community Hall?

JED: That'll be nice.

SALLY: I never liked fireworks. The smell of sulphur makes me sick. I wouldn't look very patriotic throwing up.

KEN: Oh, any honest reaction, I think. (WESTON, *on the porch, is playing a soft melody on the guitar*)

SALLY: (*At the screen door*) It's gonna rain on Harley Campbell's funeral tomorrow. It must have rained every vacation we came down here. I don't know why Matt loved it. Everyone hated him. If it rained, he went fishing. Never caught a fish. I don't think he baited his hook. Loved every minute of it. Hated catching fish. Didn't want the responsibility. Sat in the rain and laughed like a moron. They all must have thought he was mad.

KEN: Don't be absurd; he was as sane as you.

SALLY: (*Looking out the door*) Where have they got to now? They came back from town.

KEN: They went into their room, shut the door, and are, we presume, going at it.

SALLY: Again? He certainly does try very hard to keep her occupied, doesn't he?

KEN: John has always known what side he was buttered on.

SALLY: You get the feeling the moment they're alone if she opens her mouth and doesn't sing, he sticks something in it. Was he like that when you lived with them?

JUNE: I didn't live with them, Kenny lived with them.

KEN: June moved out; if you can't stand the heat, get out of the kitchen.

JUNE: The heat didn't bother me; it was the smell of all those burning cookies. (KEN *starts the tape recorder, the mangled words are heard again*) I've been meaning to tell you that's really my favorite thing to listen to.

SALLY: Is there a moon tonight?

JUNE: I think that and Mahler are in a class by themselves.

SALLY: He loved swimming naked.

KEN: Mahler? Loved swimming naked?

SALLY: Your Uncle Matt, darling.

KEN: Gustav (my time will come) Mahler, can you imagine it?

JUNE: Who is that, anyway?

KEN: This kid's name is Johnny Young. He's at the junior high. Wouldn't be in my class for years. And don't smirk, he's got an IQ of about 200. At noon tomorrow I'm supposed to tell this kid what I thought of his story.

JUNE: That's a story? I could tell you now.

KEN: He's kind of amazing. He's into the future.

JUNE: God, that entire Young family scared me to death. I'd walk a mile out of my way not to pass that house.

SALLY: Who did?

JUNE: You remember the Young brood. The church was always taking food baskets to them.

KEN: That they promptly sold.

JUNE: Four hundred white-haired children, all beautiful. All vacant as a jar. A snaggle-toothed old crone out in the back yard, literally stirring a bubbling caldron. Grinning through the steam, cackling like a hen.

SALLY: She was making soap.

JUNE: Ummm . . . Sure, she was making soap. But out of what?

KEN: Oh, he's impossible. (*Turns it off. He gets up, taking a crutch in each hand, and crosses to another chair*) He's more than likely a mathematical prodigy. No one here is qualified to judge. He communicates by scribbled messages. Half his problem is just tension. Fear of being anticipated. Everyone has cut him off as soon as they get the gist of what he's trying to say for so long that—

JUNE: Okay, okay . . .

KEN: (*He glares. She smiles*) He had almost no control over his entire vocal apparatus when we started. Nothing more than tension, really. He was simply terrified.

JED: Pissed his pants.

KEN: Not since that first time, actually.

JUNE: Oh, fine.

KEN: Entirely my fault. I couldn't understand the son of a bitch was asking for permission to go to the john.

JUNE: You're terrific.

KEN: The patience of Job.

JUNE: (*Exiting*) What a mother you would have been.

KEN: Was Job a good mother?

SALLY: June is being an awful tart, isn't she?

KEN: June is even more impossible with a straight man in the house than she is without one.

SALLY: I don't know why she had to come down here with me.

KEN: Oh, don't you?

SALLY: That's over long ago, surely.

KEN: You know that, and I know that . . .

SALLY: But where would that get her?

KEN: Nevertheless.

SALLY: Well, it gives her focus. Poor June. You were always so bright and so popular, June was always rather "The Cheese Stands Alone." (*At the desk*) What's this?

KEN: It isn't on the desk, Aunt Sally. Please don't start. Where are your glasses?

SALLY: I don't know. My glasses are being an awful child today. How are you feeling? You don't look well at all.

KEN: I'm not well at all. (*To* JED) Is that the pest book?

JED: Mildew.

SALLY: Mildew? Not on the roses.

JED: Sally, bite your tongue.

SALLY: How do you know so much about gardening? Did you grow up on a farm?

KEN: No, darling, he has a Master's in botany.

JED: And no botanist has ever known anything at all about gardening, or there wouldn't be mildew on the phlox.

SALLY: Mildew on the phlox . . . What's the name of that novel?

JOHN: (*Off*) I'll kill her; you kidding me? (*Entering; elated*) Hey, you sneak! Where is she? Hey, you know in Europe you could have your eyes poked out for something like that? Caught the little twerp at the window. You're really going to get it. She was looking in the—

SHIRLEY: (*Appearing at the door*) I certainly hope you aren't addressing me.

JOHN: How's that for innocence?

SHIRLEY: I have no idea—

SHIRLEY: —what you are making such a disturbance about, but if you are alluding to me, there are any number of low and sniggling people who might do something of that kind.

JOHN: You little sneak. You peeper. If you don't watch out, I'll tell it all. You could get yourself in a pack of trouble. That wasn't just snorting a little coke and smoking dope like last night . . .

SHIRLEY: I have no memory of last night and I am a minor and not responsible for the delinquency that so-called majors are leading me into.

KEN: What are you got up as?

JUNE: She makes about as good a drag as you would.

KEN: Anything is possible with a little taste and charm.

SHIRLEY: This is a beautiful gown that my great-grandmother wore when—

JUNE: She's been at Grandma's trunk in the attic.

KEN: You look like some drunken deb in a *Look* magazine photo essay . . .

SHIRLEY: I have never in my life heard of *Look* magazine. I have never in my life heard of most of the things you talk about.

KEN: That is hardly any fault of mine. (GWEN *enters, wearing only a sheet*)

SHIRLEY: And you are a degenerate, is what you are. Yes, I was looking in the window and I was smoking a cigarette and I have never seen anything so disgusting in my entire life. He didn't even have his shoes off! He didn't even have his pants down! He was fully dressed and Gwen was fully naked! And he was performing cunnilingus all over her and his face was all over mucus and it was the most disgusting thing I've ever seen in my life. And worse, worse, worse, she was moaning and groaning and he—he—he was reaching down with his own hand and masturbating his own thing at the same time. Himself! I have never seen anything so unnatural

JOHN: You are too much; and she was also smoking a cigarette, weren't you? When did you start that? And she was spying on a private act, weren't you? I think you ought to learn a lesson. I think you should learn a thing or two . . . You better watch it. You're asking for it . . . You watch it. You better just watch it. You're gonna get it now. That's it. You've had it. (*He continues*)

GWEN: Oh, I was! It was too fantastic! Oh, God, we were caught in the act! It was too fantastic. I looked back and saw this face at the window. Oh, shit, spies. No, audience! Oh, God, how fabulous. And like, wow, I really hit the moon. I mean I came like a flash! I've never come like that in such a flash in my life. I just went flash! Flash! All my blood, like, just went

and warped in my young life! flash! All through my body.
Ever!   You were terrific! Shirley,
                                               you gotta always be there!

(JOHN *has continued saying "I'll get you for this. You just see.
I'm gonna really get you for this"*)

SHIRLEY: You just try it. You keep your dirty hands off me.
(*Yells when he would touch her*)

JUNE: (*Overlapping*) John, Shirley, Shirley. You are going to
rip that dress that does not belong to you. And you are
forgetting that this evening is rather a sober occasion for
some people if it isn't for you. Try for one night to respect
Aunt Sally and Uncle Matt.

GWEN: Oh, shit. I forgot! I've got to dress. Don't anybody
leave without me. (*Runs off*)

SALLY: If he's waited over a year, he can wait a little longer.

SHIRLEY: I have just seen something that will warp my
young mind and all you can think of is death and ashes.
And I love Aunt Sally, whom I consider my mother, and
Uncle Matt, who was the only father I ever had, a good
deal more than—

JUNE: I'm gonna bust your ass for you, too, honey, if you try
to dump that guilt trip on me.

SHIRLEY: I will not be a party to casting my dear granduncle's
ashes into some filthy swimming hole, because I have more
respect for his memory than that.

JUNE: I'm going to dump you in the river, which is something
I should have done when I had the chance.

JOHN: You better watch that one. She's gettin' a little big for her pants, ain't you? How old are you now? How old are you?

JUNE: You wouldn't know, of course.

SHIRLEY: Age is the most irrelevant judge of character or maturity that—

JOHN: Yeah, yeah, how old are you?

JUNE: She's thirteen.

SHIRLEY: I am nineteen and I will be twenty next month.

JUNE: She's thirteen.

SHIRLEY: I am eighteen years old, and it is none of your business . . .

JUNE: She's thirteen.

SHIRLEY: I'm seventeen. If you must know.

JUNE: You are not seventeen, you cretin.

SHIRLEY: I will be seventeen in less than twenty-five days. I will!

JUNE: She's thirteen.

SHIRLEY: I am fifteen years old!

JUNE: She's fourteen. (JOHN *picks* SHIRLEY *up and carries her over his shoulder to the porch and slams the door on her. All through this, she is screaming: "Put me down, put me down, Rhett Butler, put me down"*)

JOHN: (*Smiles, turns back to the bedroom*) Yeah? You better watch that one. (*Exits to his bedroom*)

SHIRLEY: (*Comes back in, follows him to steps*) I happen to, am going to be an artist, and an artist has no age and must force himself to see everything, no matter how disgusting and how low! (*Door slams; offstage*)

WESTON: (*Pause*) Far out.

KEN: (*Pause*) I'm terribly sorry, Wes, what is it that's far out?

WESTON: The dude's been dead over a year?

SALLY: Oh, I know, I just don't get things done.

KEN: It isn't as though he'd spoil.

SALLY: No, the dear, they won't spoil.

SHIRLEY: Oh, God. Oh, my God!

JUNE: Will you please get out of that dress and stop trying to be the center of attention . . . (*Indicates bedroom*) That was cute. Wasn't he cute?

KEN: We always thought so.

WESTON: He wanted you to scatter his ashes on the water?

JUNE: He said flush them down the toilet.

SALLY: Matt's wishes were never expressed.

JUNE: But we're taking him to the river. Better late than never.

KEN: It's hardly the Ganges, but you go with what you've got . . .

WESTON: Sure.

SALLY: All he said was don't keep my ashes in a goddamned urn.

SHIRLEY: Oh, Jesus, God, I—ughh.

SALLY: But one thing and another . . .

WESTON: Far out.

SHIRLEY: I cannot bear it. I am a religious person. I happen to . . .

JUNE: If you please . . .

SALLY: Well, of course the funeral home gave him to me in an enormous, blue, hermetically sealed urn with *Matt Friedman* in gold Old English lettering. I certainly took him out of that and put him in a box.

WESTON: Sure.

SHIRLEY: I cannot bear mature people calmly talking about cremation and death and ashes in a box. I cannot bear it.

SALLY: I open it up every day and give him a little air.

WESTON: Sure.

JUNE: Wes, don't start her off.

SHIRLEY: I cannot bear it.

SALLY: I dried a rose in him last week. Dried it very nicely, too. You know, Jed discovered this lost rose.

JED: Slater's Crimson China.

SALLY: Hybrid perpetual.

JED: China Tea.

SALLY: He made a very good drying agent, too.

JUNE: He would have had a fit.

KEN: Actually, he might be put to better use spread around the rosebushes as fertilizer.

JED: Potash, absolutely. Prevents dieback.

KEN: Or John's ashes should be good for a quantity of potash, if you think about it . . .

JED: You cremate John and I'll happily spread his ashes.

SHIRLEY: I will absolutely *scream* if anyone says "ashes" one more time.

SALLY: I suppose the river is as good a place for him as any. He used to fish there. And we made love there the first time.

JUNE: Do we have to wait for those two?

SHIRLEY: That's where they saw the UFO from.

SALLY: No, it was not. We were standing right on that porch when we saw the UFO.

WESTON: You've sighted UFO's here? I read this book about flying saucers.

JUNE: Don't start her . . . Wes, you read too much, concentrate on your music.

SALLY: We went out onto the porch. This was only our second date, mind. Only it wasn't *that* porch, because the back of the house had been let go, so we had to watch where we stepped.

WESTON: Sure.

SALLY: And we saw this silver thing . . . rise straight up from the river down there. Very slowly, till it was just over the trees. Just this huge lit-up top. And then it went off sideways —phettt! and was gone—just like nothing.

WESTON: Did it go "phettt!"?

SALLY: No. I went "phettt!" It didn't go anything.

JUNE: A marriage made in heaven, right?

WESTON: There's a saucer-shaped one and a cigar-shaped one. Only they think the cigar-shaped one is just the saucer-shaped one seen on an ellipse, like. Did it have a tail?

SALLY: No, no tail.

WESTON: Some of them have tails.

SALLY: This one didn't have a tail.

WESTON: Some of them don't have tails.

SALLY: This was one of the ones that didn't have a tail.

WESTON: Some of them don't have tails.

SALLY: Well, I mean to tell you, I wet my pants.

WESTON: Sure.

JUNE: You were lucky.

SALLY: I did. I wet my pants. Of course, we thought we were being invaded by the Japanese.

WESTON: Sure.

SALLY: We got on the telephone to the Civil Defense and they said to stay away from the area, don't go down there. Of course we were down there in a minute.

WESTON: Sure.

SALLY: And, well, all the weeds and brush all along our river-bank were burned away. The place was still smoldering.

WESTON: Sure.

SHIRLEY: Probably they were burned by all kinds of radiation.

KEN: That would explain a good deal.

SALLY: And we ran all up and down the river, looking for spies, and listening, because that's what we thought it was. That they had landed Jap—Japanese troops.

WESTON: Sure.

SALLY: And by the time we had gone all the way to the boathouse we had to rest, and we talked and looked at the moon, and I'm afraid we got all involved with each other and forgot about the Japanese.

KEN: With wet pants? I'm sorry.

SALLY: Isn't that funny? I completely forgot what I did about that. Of course, no one had any idea what it was we had seen. It was years yet before anyone started talking about UFO's.

WESTON: Sure.

SALLY: But every time we came down here, every year after that, we went out to watch for them.

SHIRLEY: That's probably why Uncle Matt kept coming back down here.

JUNE: Shirley, are you going to go or are you going to stay, because you can't go looking like that.

SHIRLEY: I have said repeatedly that I was staying here, and the sooner we get back to St. Louis and you stop acting like a mother the happier I'll be.

JUNE: Just a simple decision, we don't need the production number.

SHIRLEY: Unlike either of you, I do not have a single memory of the boyfriends I dated during the war in this one-horse burg.

JUNE: Where do you get the way you talk? I did not have "boyfriends," we did not go on "dates": haven't you learned anything? She spends twenty-four hours a day in the queer movie house, watching Betty Grable reruns.

SHIRLEY: Betty Grable is the greatest star Missouri ever produced.

KEN: Oh, God. I'll bet that's true.

SHIRLEY: I would think one would know better than to proclaim her chastity to her illegitimate daughter.

JUNE: There is a world of difference between making love and teasing some basketball player after the junior prom.

KEN: June certainly never teased anyone.

SHIRLEY: That from a woman who has written, "The truly *liberated* person is free in mind, not in body," on the wall of the apartment in Magic Marker.

JUNE: I am going to cut your filthy tongue right out of your filthy face if you can't learn to respect people's aspirations! (GWEN *enters, dressed flamboyantly*)

KEN: Holy God.

GWEN: I decided, if Shirley is wearing that, I'd let her set the tone.

JED: (*To* KEN) Be a minute; hold down the fort. (*Exits upstairs*)

JUNE: She isn't going, and she certainly isn't wearing that.

SALLY: (*Overlapping*) Now, where did you get to? You were here last night, and what did I do with you? It was hot—I know that.

KEN: (*Overlapping*) Has anybody seen Aunt Sally's roll of copper wire?

GWEN: What brand? Copper's my business.

SALLY: What? Oh, yes, but no, darling, Uncle Matt. I can't seem to remember what I've done with his box of ashes.

KEN: (KEN *and* JUNE *at the same time, overlapping*) Don't say it!

JUNE: Please don't! (SHIRLEY *screams*)

WESTON: (*Pause*) Far out.

GWEN: Oh, God, that's so great. I'd be a new person if I could do that. Ever since my shrink told me I should scream, I haven't been able to.

JUNE: Don't pay any attention to her. She's only trying to be the center of—oh, God, I sound exactly like Dad, don't I?

KEN: His voice was higher.

JUNE: Men and women aren't strong enough to have children. Trees should have children.

KEN: I'm afraid I can't help you, Aunt Sally. I haven't seen them.

SALLY: (*Overlapping*) I only have to concentrate a moment. I had them last night, when it was so warm, and I took them up to the bedroom, but I don't remember bringing him down this morning. I remember it was so hot and Matt always hated that. Used to go into the guest room, said I was like a furnace. Loved it in the winter because it saved on heating fuel, couldn't stand it in the summer. That's why—

KEN: (*Yelling upstairs*) Jed! Hey, Jed!

GWEN: That's so wonderful.

JED: (*Yelling, offstage*) Yo!

GWEN: Jed is really butch, isn't he? Don't you love him?

KEN: (*Yelling*) Listen . . . !

GWEN: I mean he's dull as dishwater, but he's so butch!

KEN: (*Yelling*) Bring down Uncle Matt from Aunt Sally's bedroom when you come!

SALLY: No, darling, something tells me I didn't leave him up there. It was so warm, I was worried—

JED: (*Offstage*) He's in the refrigerator!

SALLY: Oh, of course he is.

WESTON: Wow, that's really—

JUNE: Don't say it. One word.

WESTON: (*Mouth open, can't close it*) I been reading this book about the Bermuda Triangle.

SHIRLEY: Oh, the Bermuda Triangle.

GWEN: Listen, forget it; it's a total rip-off. We went down there to try to disappear. Like we did everything you could think of to make ourselves conspicuous, you know? Not a fuckin' thing happened to us. Two solid months.

WESTON: There's supposed to be another one off Japan.

GWEN: Yeah, I know, they say it's even better, but I heard that's real bullshit, too.

SHIRLEY: How long are you going to be in Nashville?

GWEN: Just a couple of days. You want to come?

SHIRLEY: Yes! (JUNE *starts to leave the room*)

SALLY: Where are you going?

JUNE: I'm . . . going to . . . the loo. You want to come?

SALLY: Just leave Matt in the refrigerator. He's fine there. (JUNE *stops, stares*)

JUNE: (*To* KEN) You can shrug it off, right?

KEN: Don't push, don't force it.

JUNE: You're the only person I know who can say "I'm not involved" in forty-five languages.

KEN: Seven or eight.

SHIRLEY: You got to really know the Caribbean, though—

GWEN: You don't want to know the Caribbean, believe me. They're on their fifteenth replacement cast down there. I got dysentery, spent three weeks in the hospital; and that was a trip, too, believe me—

SHIRLEY: The only place I've ever been for a vacation is Lebanon.

GWEN: Oh, shit. That's probably the pits, right? We were in Egypt, the guide stands in front of the Sphinx; he says, "For five thousand years the Sphinx has not given up her secret. Command her to speak but she remains silent." I said, you gotta be runnin' that up my ass, right?

KEN: Lebanon, Missouri.

SHIRLEY: (*Overlapping*) Here; you're there now.

GWEN: Oh, listen, no, this is the greatest place I've ever been. We walked down to the river, we were up on the hill; I've never seen such peace in my life.

SHIRLEY: Every place I've ever been has been peaceful.

GWEN: No shit; I want to buy it.

SALLY: Oh, you do not.

KEN: Aunt Sally, darling.

GWEN: How much land is there?

KEN: About twenty acres; a little under that.

SALLY: Isn't that pitiful? That's how Buddy backed his mobile homes. A hundred acres here, a hundred and fifty there—

GWEN: Well, it isn't like we wanted to raise goats. John, dammit, come in here a minute. (*To* WESTON) What do you think? We could put in the studio, you know?

WESTON: Where?

GWEN: Pick a room, Christ, there must be thirty rooms.

JUNE: Nineteen.

GWEN: Yeah, nineteen. Pick one.

JOHN: (*Offstage*) What say, baby?

GWEN: Come in here, you look great.

JOHN: (*Entering*) Okay, I'm clean.

SHIRLEY: Don't touch me, I don't care.

JOHN: She's really gonna get it. What's up?

GWEN: When would we be here? Like spring, part of the summer, right? I think we could make something out of it. It's close enough to Nashville without being in their laps. We could hop over there; there's room for the band to live here. It's quiet as a tomb. You couldn't ask for a better setup. We got to have our own place to record, see, 'cause the studios bleed you dry. You wouldn't believe it.

WESTON: Oh, wow, and she's . . .

JOHN: Gwen's got a little problem; we're working on . . . It runs into a lot of bread.

WESTON: She gets blocks.

SALLY: She gets what?

WESTON: Blocks. You know, like mental blocks.

KEN: Sally!

JOHN: It's like the same thing with learning to drive a car. She'd be a good driver, but she gets it all going right and everything, except she keeps forgetting to look out the window.

KEN: Beautiful.

JOHN: And with recording, see, it all goes fine till they turn on the mikes.

GWEN: Fuck it, it's not that bad.

JOHN: Listen, I thought it was cool.

WESTON: She freezes.

JOHN: She freezes. Her jaws clench up.

WESTON: You can't even pry them open with your fingers. We tried. It's really a bitch.

GWEN: Just to cut two sides I'm probably the only singer ever spent more money on the shrink than we did on the band.

JOHN: It was cool. The band sat around, we ordered in these hams, we had beer, we had barbecue ribs, they didn't seem to mind.

WESTON: They hung around 'cause we didn't know when she'd unlock.

KEN: How long did it take?

JOHN: About two weeks.

KEN: Who's paying for all that?

GWEN: Oh, fine, rub it in.

JOHN: The band was really great, though.

GWEN: 'Cause they had decided I was just this rich bitch, you know, but like when we finally got it together they really flipped. Like they said I got this real pain in my voice.

KEN: It isn't much, but it's a start, right?

GWEN: Well, let's face it, like if I don't have pain in my voice, who would?

JOHN: There had to have been something to impress Jimmy King. Sent the first tape we did to Jimmy King.

GWEN: Who's like the top manager in the business. They don't know Jimmy King.

JOHN: He wants to sign them both.

GWEN: Only thing he said I really should concentrate on this one thing and like what happens to the copper business?

JOHN: One thing at a time, one thing at a time.

GWEN: Only I'm never sure which time to take what thing.

JOHN: You gotta learn to think about yourself.

GWEN: But wouldn't that be far out to have this really major career after you're already thirty-three years old and burned out?

JOHN: Nobody says you're burned—

GWEN: Everybody says I'm burned out. How can you take that many drugs and go through what I've gone through and not have your brains fried?

SHIRLEY: You are *thirty-three years old?*

GWEN: Isn't that gross? I mean, like really scary-time. Like the crucifixion bit and all that.

SHIRLEY: I couldn't possibly live to be thirty.

GWEN: You always think that, but then you do. (KEN *presses the recorder*)

SHIRLEY: No, you don't understand, Gwen, my candle burns at both—

GWEN: Oh, God, I was gonna tell you. That's really weird to make love to.

JOHN: You've got your work cut out for you, if this is one of your English students.

KEN: No, no, when I was in the hospital learning to walk, I worked with a couple of guys who had lost their ability to speak. Mac McConnell wanted me to work with this kid privately to see if I could help him.

JUNE: Johnny Young. Remember the Young brood?

JOHN: Jesus, forget I mentioned it. When do you start again, September?

JUNE: Funny you should ask.

KEN: Start what?

GWEN: Teaching.

KEN: Oh, hardly, no. The profession has done very nicely without me for six years, I think it will survive a while longer.

GWEN: What the hell are you talking about? I thought that's what you were down here for. You were going back to your old high school.

KEN: I was never that interested in teaching.

SALLY: Oh, you were so.

GWEN: (*Overlapping* SALLY) You used to scream about it all the time.

JOHN: Hell you weren't, that was your mission, I thought.

KEN: Well, once again, SuperFag's plans fail to materialize.

JOHN: That guy said you were the best teacher Oakland ever had.

KEN: (*Suddenly unleashing his pent-up tension*) Would you get off my back? That's all I hear from Jed and Sally and June. I don't need it from you. Yes, I was quite happy leaving our cozy abode in Oakland each morning and walking briskly into the Theodore Roosevelt High School. Very "Good Morning, Miss Dove"; very "Goodbye, Mr. Chips." And—by prancing and dancing and sleight of hand, I actually managed to get their attention off sex for one hour a day. They became quite fascinated by trochees, thrilled by Cyrano de Bergerac. But now I'm afraid my prancing would be quite embarrassing to them.

JOHN: So you're afraid, so you'll get over it.

JUNE: Running like a rabbit would be closer—

KEN: (*Almost angry*) Fear has nothing to do with it. As I slowly realized that no accredited English Department was interested in my stunningly overqualified application, except the notoriously parochial home town—

JUNE: Fine, that's where you belong.

KEN: —I became aware that what everyone was trying to tell me was—that teaching impressionable teenagers in my present state, I could only expect to leave quite the wrong impression. You have no idea how much noise I make falling down.

JOHN: Oh, bull. A big-deal war hero. They'd love you.

KEN: I don't think so. And though it seems incredible to us, they don't even know where Vietnam is.

JUNE: Why don't you just admit you're vain and terrified and face it instead of—

KEN: I have simply developed an overpowering distaste for chalk.

JUNE: Also, the idiot has been up in St. Louis all winter, trying to prove his independence. He's gotten completely out of shape and he's back in physical therapy.

KEN: I only go twice a week.

GWEN: Yeah, and—?

KEN: This nice dyke nurse tries to kill me. It's this game we play.

JOHN: I thought you were finished with all that.

GWEN: Why are you back in muscular therapy, creep?

KEN: Good God, no reason. Apparently I was walking wrong. I was walking with my arms instead of my stomach.

JOHN: Well, okay, teaching is the only thing you ever said you wanted to do with your life. You obviously don't want to do that any more. What do you want to do? Huh? What you got in mind to do with yourself?

KEN: Yeah. (*Yelling upstairs*) Jed. Let's go. Come on!

JUNE: Calling in the dogs, right?

KEN: No more. That's it!

JOHN: Come on, off your butt, we're gonna travel.

WESTON: Goin' where?

JOHN: We're gonna do the Matt Friedman gig; then we're gonna see my home town's Fourth of July bash.

WESTON: No way.

GWEN: Honey . . . ?

JOHN: Big deal, get off your butt, get some air.

WESTON: I been getting air all day—I've never seen so much air in my life.

JUNE: They don't have air in New Jersey?

WESTON: They got something, but it ain't air.

JOHN: He hasn't been home in two years.

GWEN: Honey, maybe I should stay here, 'cause Wes and me have to work, you know.

JOHN: No, we'll all go; we'll go on to the fireworks. You know if you don't go you'll be disappointed later.

GWEN: I just came here to see Kenny, I didn't bargain for funerals.

JUNE: It won't be like that at all.

JOHN: When you chicken out, you're always sorry later—

GWEN: Come on, I can't do it. I thought I could 'cause he was so nice, but I'm going to freak out. I just keep thinking about my daddy and my brother and I'm gonna freak. Tell me it isn't ashes. Tell me it's something else.

KEN: It's something else.

GWEN: No, no, you know, Johnny. Tell me it's something else. Make it better.

JOHN: Baby, you're thinking about your old man. You can't think about him. He's fine. The last time I saw him, he was—

GWEN: No, no, no, you're trying to change the subject; it's not gonna work to change the subject. You've gotta tell me it's something else.

JUNE: It's pickled peaches. We're going down to the river, we're going to have a picnic, we'll—

GWEN: —No, no, God, no, not something to eat! Tell me— oh, God, I'm going to freak out. I'm really gonna freak.

JOHN: Baby, you don't have to do a thing you don't want to.

KEN: Gwen. I do not know why you are carrying on. Have you seen that box? Have you seen it?

GWEN: No.

KEN: Well, do you know what's in it?

GWEN: No.

KEN: Well, you know while I was in the hospital I got all these presents from people who don't go to hospitals—you know that.

GWEN: People are such creeps! People are so candy-ass.

KEN: Well, you remember all the chocolates I got—

GWEN: We brought you angel dust, we didn't bring you—

KEN: But others, granted, less enterprising. You remember all those chocolates?

GWEN: Yeah, we sat on your bed and punched the bottoms out of them.

KEN: And half of them were something vile like—what was it you don't like?

GWEN: . . . maple.

KEN: I hate jelly chocolates.

GWEN: Oh, God, I hate jelly chocolates.

KEN: Well, that box is filled to the top with a six-year sup-ply of jelly chocolates with their bottoms pushed in. And we are finally going to feed that crap to the fish.

GWEN: Maybe somebody likes—

KEN: Nobody likes jelly chocolates.

GWEN: Oh, God, I hate it.

KEN: The fish will love it.

GWEN: Why don't you just throw them in the garbage?

KEN: It's against the law.

GWEN: Fuck 'em. Throw it in the garbage. (JED *enters, in a suit*)

JOHN: We thought we'd make a party of it.

GWEN: So you go on to the party and Wes and I'll stay here.

JOHN: You know I'm not going to leave you. We go or we stay, I don't care.

GWEN: You come back for us after you've dumped the candy.

JUNE: Fine, now. Aunt Sally, can we do this?

SALLY: I'll go, June. Kenny said don't push me. You always push. (*Exits downstairs,* JUNE *follows her off*)

JOHN: They don't need this friction, honey, they're having a little problem.

GWEN: Well, I'm having a little problem, too. I don't believe for a minute it's candy in that box; I know perfectly well who's in there. (SHIRLEY *enters from upstairs, wearing a different dress*) Oh, that's fabulous.

SHIRLEY: I had it made for me in Paris.

JOHN: You and me will stay here with Wes and Shirley.

GWEN: You should go.

JOHN: I better not go without you; you'll decide to come and not know how to get there. (*Phone rings*)

KEN: That's long-distance.

JOHN: I'll get it, it's gonna be for us.

JED: (*Has picked up the phone*) Please do.

JOHN: No, no, please.

JED: It's person-to-person. (*Hands phone to* JOHN, *goes upstairs*)

SHIRLEY: (*To* GWEN) He never leaves you alone for a minute. (JUNE *reenters*)

JUNE: (*To* KEN) She's talking to him, for God's sake.

KEN: Well, why not? Wouldn't you?

GWEN: Listen, they're gonna dump the candy and then they're coming back for us and we're all going to the Independence dance, do you love it?

SHIRLEY: No. Being a woman, I feel any display of independence at this—

JUNE: You're going to get read a lecture, if that's what you want.

GWEN: She sounds exactly like you. Jesus Christ, that was fourteen years ago.

SHIRLEY: I sound like me and no one else!

GWEN: Does anybody want a Quaalude? I'm really freaking out. (*Yelling*) John, if that's that prick in Nashville, I want to talk with him.

JOHN: I've got it, I've got it. It's cool, it's cool. Soon as I'm finished.

SHIRLEY: I am not going to attend a so-called fireworks display—

GWEN: Fireworks! I love 'em—the tackier, the better.

KEN: Darling, the town of Lebanon is not ready for you freaking out at their Independence Day celebration. That independent they aren't.

GWEN: Bullshit; if they can take you, they can take anything.

KEN: Don't be absurd. I have short hair and I'm a war vet. I am pathetic and brave and I've paid my dues. They even want me to teach their children *Wuthering Heights*. (*Looks at* JUNE *a moment*)

JUNE: I don't know if she's going to do this tonight or not.

KEN: Well, it's all up to her.

GWEN: (*To* SHIRLEY, *who has* GWEN*'s pillbox*) You better not take one of those.

JUNE: Oh, let her have one.

SHIRLEY: I was merely trying to examine the pillbox.

GWEN: Yeah, but like one day you're trying to look at the box and the next day you're burned out and your hair won't hold a permanent.

SHIRLEY: How did you get burned out?

GWEN: Listen, I'm a real case, no shit. Like a year doesn't go by without me getting something terminal wrong with me.

WESTON: She's got this history of like medical milestone operations—

SHIRLEY: Oh, no.

GWEN: It's really crazy; I mean, I'm this fuckin' shell. They took everything out by the time I was twenty-five. You know, not all at once, one or two things at a time.

SHIRLEY: Oh, Lord . . .

GWEN: If I didn't have this history of longevity in my family, I'd've been dead before I was ten.

WESTON: But like nobody in her family dies.

GWEN: Like you got to kill us off. Daddy's been like paralyzed, you know, for the last four years, with all these tubes and wires and all, but—I mean, like he's a Brussels sprout, but he's alive. It'd be really tragic, but you can't think about it without laughing, 'cause you know he had this stroke—

SHIRLEY: Oh. I cannot bear it.

GWEN: No, listen, it's far out. His face is all paralyzed, you know, but it's stuck in this real weird comic position. I mean even Matt Friedman, who was like the most serious person I know, had to leave the room to keep from cracking up.

WESTON: She's got this real tragic history.

GWEN: Ask Wes.

WESTON: Her mother and her brother were killed in an airplane crash.

GWEN: Ronny, it was too bad; Mom was a bitch. (*Pause*) I don't want to be a down or anything. (JOHN *hangs up the phone*) You didn't hang up? I wanted to talk to him.

JOHN: No, it was just the engineer, checking our schedule.

GWEN: You haven't talked to Schwartzkoff, have you?

JOHN: I thought he went on vacation.

GWEN: No, the creep. I know damn well he's gonna call another meeting: every time I leave L.A., he calls the board. The last time I went to the hospital, I was having like my spleen stripped—

KEN: Hardly that—

GWEN: Well, who remembers, the son of a bitch called a meeting of the board to stab me in the back. He votes Daddy's stock, I can't vote it.

SHIRLEY: A stripped spleen?

KEN: Cassandra had it easy, you don't want to know.

GWEN: Cassandra? Oh, shit, don't you wish you knew all those myths? Like way down in some primordial place I've got this intuition that it's all in the myths, all the answers, if we could just get it together right.

WESTON: I was up in Canada, I got this book of Eskimo folk tales.

GWEN: I had this numerologist from South America, he was such a dopehead—I mean, he was like the original Peruvian flake, but the one true thing he said was it's all in the myths. I really believe that.

JUNE: Do you think we could go now, while nobody's freaking out?

JOHN: The Eskimos are in Alaska.

WESTON: No, they're both; they're in Canada, too. Did you know igloos aren't warm?

KEN: I hadn't thought about it before, but it makes sense.

WESTON: They're below freezing.

KEN: If it were above freezing, igloos would melt, wouldn't they?

WESTON: They have these blubber-oil lamps and these fur blankets and each other to keep themselves warm, and that's all.

JUNE: I'm sorry, I don't find that romantic at all.

GWEN: What's an Eskimo myth about?

WESTON: They're mostly about blubber. They're really these strange people. Like, they think very different from the way we think.

JOHN: I don't think I've ever been interested in the Eskimos, have you?

KEN: I don't think I have.

WESTON: There's this one folk story about this family. They had all this caribou meat stacked outside their igloo. Frozen, see. But it got so cold that their whole winter's supply of meat was frozen in one solid block of ice and none of the family could get at it. And they were all starving, 'cause no one could break off any of this meat. So in a kind of last-ditch heroic effort this young Eskimo warrior goes outside and lets off this tremendous, powerful fart.

SHIRLEY: Oh, God.

WESTON: And thaws all the meat.

JUNE: That is very gross.

WESTON: But it stank so bad none of the family could eat it. And they all starved to death.

SHIRLEY: Oh, God.

KEN: This isn't, I hope, the basis for one of your songs.

JOHN: What kind of story is that supposed to be?

GWEN: I never heard that. Where did you hear that?

JUNE: That is gross.

WESTON: Isn't that gross?

JOHN: I mean, what kind of story is that?

WESTON: It's a folk story. It's in this book.

JUNE: Even for an Eskimo.

JOHN: That isn't a folk tale. Ken, have you ever heard a folk tale like that?

KEN: Never. And I never wanted to.

WESTON: It is. That story has been handed down from father to son, generation to generation, verbally, for hundreds of years.

SHIRLEY: Oh, God.

KEN: That isn't a folk tale, because there's no—

JOHN: What's the moral? There's no moral.

KEN: Exactly.

JOHN: Folk tales have morals. There's no moral. There's no point . . .

WESTON: They couldn't eat the meat, so they starved to death.

JOHN: They were starving to death before he farted on the damn caribou meat.

WESTON: Well, then the moral is that that isn't the way to thaw caribou meat.

JOHN: No one could. It couldn't happen.

KEN: And if it could, it is not particularly beneficial.

JOHN: Heroic actions must have saving results.

WESTON: Who says?

KEN: It is the law of folk tales.

JOHN: It's the law of heroes.

WESTON: Saving results for whom?

JOHN: For everybody. Like the little Dutch boy, for God's sake.

WESTON: Well, maybe these people are more realistic than the Greeks or the Dutch.

JOHN: It isn't realistic. It couldn't happen.

JUNE: And it's gross.

JOHN: And if it could happen, what do we learn from it? We have to learn something from a folk tale.

KEN: That's a fable, but for the sake of argument.

WESTON: We learn that that isn't the way to thaw caribou meat.

JOHN: Who cares how to thaw caribou meat?

WESTON: The Eskimo cares! It's his staple diet!

JUNE: You are certifiable, you know that?

WESTON: I said it was this alien mind.

JOHN: This is the sort of thing you read in your own time.

KEN: Where did you find him, anyway?

WESTON: Skip it.

JOHN: No, you brought it up. I think it's very interesting. I mean the story is ridiculous, but that you read it I find very interesting.

KEN: And retained it.

WESTON: Skip it. You obviously don't have the sensitivity to appreciate—

SHIRLEY: I have nothing but sensitivity and I don't even understand it.

WESTON: I thought it was a funny story to have been handed down from generation—

JOHN: I don't find it funny at all. I see it as a tragedy. The entire family dies in the snow of starvation.

WESTON: They were dying already.

JOHN: That's what I said. It is a pointless, vulgar—

KEN: Scatological—

JOHN: —scatological story.

WESTON: I only thought it was interesting because it is a completely different culture.

JOHN: Wes, that isn't culture. That's hardship.

WESTON: No, no, it is. It's an alien culture. Like they call themselves *"The* People" and everybody else is "The *Other* People."

KEN: Wes, every people call themselves "The People," and everyone else is the other people.

WESTON: They have fifty different words for snow! (*Pause*) You don't think that shows a subtle mind?

KEN: (*Pause*) Wes, of course they have fifty different words for snow.

JOHN: (*Pause*) Their winters are six months long.

KEN: They have nothing else to talk about.

JOHN: Snow is all there is.

KEN: They have to find some way to make it interesting.

JOHN: The Bedouins probably have fifty different words for sand.

WESTON: They probably do. They're a very interesting people. (*He slams out to the porch*)

KEN: They call themselves "The People" and . . .

JOHN: (*Yelling after him*) Wes, you know why you're not going to make a successful songwriter? Because you have too many interests.

GWEN: There's a song about syphilis, though; songs can be about anything. (JED *comes downstairs with a bottle of pills*)

SHIRLEY: You are so depressing.

GWEN: You want to smoke some dope?

SHIRLEY: I never again want any foreign matter in my body. Last night I threw up.

GWEN: Oh, I do that all the time. After a while, you groove on it. (JED *hands* KEN *a pill, points to his watch*) What are you taking?

KEN: We get these special little birth-control pills. In my condition we can't take chances.

JED: It's Percodan. (*Pours a glass of water from his watering can*)

GWEN: That's like a horse-size painkiller.

KEN: We try to spice up our lives, what we can.

GWEN: Wouldn't that be a drag, to have to take those? At least I've got through that.

SHIRLEY: Can't you have children?

GWEN: Oh, please. That was like the first thing to go.

SHIRLEY: That's terrible . . .

GWEN: No, it's like no big deal at all. I mean, if you want children, like, my God, there are children everywhere. Actually, it was kinda fabulous because they accidentally cut a nerve and—

SHIRLEY: No, no, I'm going to bed, I can't bear it. I'm going—

GWEN: (*Overlapping*) No, no, really, no, this is good, really, listen. They cut a nerve that's connected to some sexual response thing so I feel sex like five times as intense as the normal person. Isn't that fabulous?

SHIRLEY: I never intend to have sex in my life.

GWEN: Yeah, but it isn't what you intend.

SHIRLEY: I will never have any form of—

GWEN: Never say that. You don't know what you're missing. Listen, when we heard that Kenny was wounded, Kenny, I'll bet I never told you this—like I know every doctor in the country, like half of them are drawing royalties for me, like case "G" or case "Y"—I called up, I had to go right to the head of the damn Naval Hospital in Washington, I didn't get off till he told me Kenny's sexual performance would be in no way impaired.

KEN: Depends on what I'm expected to perform.

GWEN: Don't screw around, you know what I mean, your sexual performance . . .

KEN: . . . was absolutely in no way impaired; though we have had to cut out one show a night.

GWEN: I was so thankful, I went to church and actually lit a candle.

KEN: Appropriately.

GWEN: No shit, Shirl, I put five hundred dollars in the box.

SHIRLEY: I am going to devote my life to art. The way Marie Curie devoted her life to science.

GWEN: Oh, science. I did that. I did.

JUNE: Darling, you didn't devote your life to science. You donated your body to science.

GWEN: Yeah, I got the tattoo on my foot; the whole trip.

JUNE: But then you freaked and had it removed.

GWEN: Yeah, you think that's not painful? Oh, shit, are those fireflies? (*Runs out to garden*)

SHIRLEY: Lightning bugs.

JOHN: Who's Marie Curie?

SHIRLEY: She was the only person to ever receive two Nobel Prizes for science. She was only the greatest scientist who ever lived.

JOHN: Okay, okay . . .

JUNE: Could we go now, Aunt Sally?

JOHN: Gwen can stay with Wes and Shirley.

KEN: You don't have to stay now?

JED: No, the phone call was from Schwartzkoff. He doesn't have to hang around waiting for it any more.

KEN: You running the copper business now?

JUNE: This country-Western singer crap is just to keep her mind off the copper business? That's just stardust, right?

KEN: Diversionary tactics.

JOHN: Hey, hold on, come on.

JED: Smoke gets in your eyes.

GWEN: (*Reentering*) Oh, God, "Smoke Gets in Your Eyes." I love that song. We gotta do that song.

SHIRLEY: I thought it was the engineer checking schedules.

JOHN: Come on, let's go. Before the squirt starts up again.

SHIRLEY: I am not starting up. I said I was going to be a great artist, which I have said repeatedly for the past solid year.

JUNE: With the emphasis on repeatedly.

SHIRLEY: And I am not a squirt!

JUNE: If I had it to do over again, I wouldn't give her to Aunt Sally. You live with a bat, you fly like a bat.

SHIRLEY: I don't think you were militant at all. I think you were just cross and angry.

GWEN: Are you kidding me? She was sensational.

JUNE: (*Shaken*) You have no idea of the life we led.

GWEN: Really.

JUNE: (*With difficulty controlling herself*) You've no idea of the country we almost made for you. The fact that I think it's all a crock now does not take away from what we almost achieved. (*Pause; then she runs upstairs*)

GWEN: (*To* SHIRLEY) Baby, you shouldn't—I mean, I think you're great, but you really don't tell someone that they aren't what they think they are. What's the profit?

SHIRLEY: Who?

GWEN: June was really something else. You would have been proud. It was her mom and dad made her send you to Sally. She was ready to carry you around like a flag. I mean, she was like Ma Barker or Belle Starr. She was really dangerous.

KEN: Mostly to herself.

GWEN: No, you don't know! Like they used to hitchhike to these rallies. I couldn't cut it. I couldn't bear the rejection. The first car passed me up, I was destroyed. I used to fly ahead and meet them. Also, I couldn't march 'cause I've never had a pair of shoes that were really comfortable.

JOHN: You were pretty good. She helped fire-bomb Pacific Gypsum, and it's her own company.

GWEN: One cocktail in the doorway of the building, broke about six windows.

SHIRLEY: And it was your own company?

GWEN: Oh, please, I was stoned. Who knew what we were doing? We were in TV, we were in *Time* magazine, it was a blast. Also it was such a crock, really. You go to an anti-war, end the war rally, right? You march to the White House.

JOHN: You take a taxi, but nonetheless.

GWEN: Anyway. You get there. Five hundred thousand people, speaker's platforms, signs thick as a convention, everybody's high, we're bombed, the place is mobbed, everybody's on the lawn with their shirts off, boys, girls; they're eating chicken and tacos, the signs say: End the War, Ban the Bomb, Black Power and Gay Power and Women's Lib; the Nazi Party's there, the unions, demanding jobs, they got Chicano Power and Free the POW's, and Free the Migrants, Allen Ginsberg is chanting Ommm over the loud-speakers, Coretta King is there: how straight do you have to be to see that nothing is going to come from it? But don't knock your mother, 'cause she really believed that "Power to the People" song, and that hurts.

JOHN: It's all right, baby.

SHIRLEY: (*Quietly determined*) I'm going to be the greatest artist Missouri has ever produced.

JOHN: Would that be so difficult?

SHIRLEY: The entire Midwest. What do you mean? There have been very famous people—world-famous people from —Tennessee Williams grew up in—

JOHN: Tennessee Williams is from Mississippi.

SHIRLEY: He may have been born there, but he grew up—

JOHN: And his people were from Tennessee, that's why—

SHIRLEY: He grew up not three blocks from where I live now! All his formative years!

JOHN: Okay, what do I know.

SHIRLEY: And Mark Twain. And Dreiser! And Vincent Price and Harry Truman! And Betty Grable! (GWEN, KEN, *and* JOHN *say "Grable" with her*) But me! Oh, God! Me! Me! Me! Me! I am going to be so great! Unqualified! The greatest single artist the Midwest has ever known!

JOHN: Yes, yes, doing what?

SHIRLEY: Something astonishing! Just astonishing!

JOHN: (*Overlapping*) In what field? What are you going to be?

SHIRLEY: A painter. Or a sculptor. Or a dancer! A writer! A conductor! A composer! An actress! One of the arts! People will die. Certain people will literally have cardiac arrests at the magnitude of my achievements.

JOHN: If you're going to be dancer or a composer, you might matriculate into some school before too much—

SHIRLEY: I will have you know that I intend to study for ten years, and then I will burst forth on the world. And people will be abashed!

KEN: I don't doubt it for a minute.

SHIRLEY: Amazed!

GWEN: I think you're terrific.

SHIRLEY: Astonished! At my magnitude. Oh, God! Look! Is that she? Is that SHE? *Is that she? Is it?* IT IS! IT IS SHE! IT IS SHE! AHHHHHHHHHHHHHHHHHHHH! (*She collapses on the floor.* JUNE *enters*)

JOHN: She recognized herself on the street and fainted.

SHIRLEY: (*Slowly getting to a sitting position; with great dignity*) She died dead of cardiac arrest and astonishment at the magnificence of my achievement in my chosen field. Only Shakespeare, Michelangelo, Beethoven, and Frank Lloyd Wright have raised to my heights before me.

JOHN: And Madame Curie.

SHIRLEY: Marie! Marie! She had a name of her own. Not Madame! Marie!

JUNE: (*Almost admiring*) You are something else.

SHIRLEY: (*To* JOHN) And when I first achieved my first achievements I was eleven years younger than you are now. (*She sweeps to the porch door*)

SALLY: (*Enters with an enormous chocolates box*) Shirley, the first time I remember seeing my mother she was wearing that dress. (*Pause.* SALLY *comes into the room and sits, holding the box on her lap.* SHIRLEY *sweeps out to the porch*)

GWEN: Boy, if I had been like that.

SHIRLEY: (*On the porch*) Weston, as we'll be traveling to Nashville together, I don't want you to think I haven't noticed the way you look at me. But I believe in putting everything on the line, and I could never seriously consider marrying you, Weston Hurley. All her life until she was thirty-one and married Matthew Friedman, my Aunt Sally lived with the impossible handicap of being named Sally Talley. And if I married you, I'd be Shirley Hurley. (*She runs off into the garden*)

KEN: Aunt Sally, I see you've got Uncle Matt in your lap. I don't think we should put this off.

SALLY: (*Long pause*) They all hated him because he was a Jew. Your mother, your father, my folks, the whole damn town hated him.

JUNE: He kept coming back down here.

SALLY: Oh, nothing bothered him except when it bothered me. And if it didn't bother him, it didn't bother me. He liked young people. Shirley was a joy to him. He was very concerned about Gwen. And he was very angry when Kenny lost his legs. People said he didn't like this country, because he wasn't afraid to speak his mind.

JUNE: They say a lot.

SALLY: I think they were right. I don't think he liked this country a bit. (WESTON *is heard on porch strumming "Anytime"*) No, I'm sorry, but if Gwen and John are going to buy the Talley place, then Matt doesn't belong here.

GWEN: No, don't feel that way about it.

SALLY: He'll just have to like California.

GWEN: Listen, feel free to come any time—

JED: Gwen and John are buying the place?

SALLY: (*To* JED) I want to talk to you about that.

JUNE: If you don't go tonight—

SALLY: I don't care. Everything is changed. I never said I'd dump this in the river. I want you to know that it doesn't mean anything to me; but I'm not going to dump them in the river. Not tonight. I'm tired. I'm going to bed. I've got to get up at the crack of dawn for Harley Campbell's funeral.

JUNE: Darling, if you don't go tonight, you'll think of some reason to wait the whole year again.

SALLY: You people go dance. I was ready before but I was wrong and I'm not ready now.

JUNE: Sally, you can't take that box to California. They won't let you into the state.

SALLY: I don't want you to badger me. I'm going to bed. (*Exits upstairs*)

JUNE: Well, to hell with it.

GWEN: Is Sally a little—I mean, not that everybody isn't.

KEN: She's all right.

JUNE: I don't intend to come here every year waiting for— well, you can have this visit from here on. It won't be on me.

KEN: She can pester Gwen and John. We won't be here.

JED: Where will we be?

JUNE: I told Dad I'd get her to dump the damn ashes before she came out there, if I had to dump them myself.

KEN: June.

JED: You're really going to buy the place?

GWEN: Oh, listen, if we put in an airstrip up on the hill, we wouldn't fuck up your garden, would we?

JED: No, not at all. But it takes twenty years for a garden to mature into anything; we only started three years ago; you don't have to follow through with it—do anything you want.

GWEN: Hell, no, we can hire gardeners.

JOHN: Write down what you got in mind. We'll do it.

JED: I'm going to change if it's off for tonight.

KEN: Might as well. Hey, we'll talk. (JED *is gone*)

JUNE: How long before you manage to sidle out of that, too?

KEN: Actually, my lateral movement is somewhat inhibited any more.

JOHN: What say we check out the fairgrounds? Hey, look at this. Just the four of us. How about that.

JUNE: Son of a bitch; together again.

GWEN: Oh, Jesus, I loved the four of us. That was like the greatest period of my life.

JUNE: Let's don't rerun that again. I couldn't take it.

GWEN: You should have stayed with us; we had like our own little commune . . .

KEN: No. Four is too large for a ménage, too small for a commune. Eventually John would have cracked under the strain of all three of us chasing his tail.

JUNE: No, it was all a little too steamy for me.

JOHN: Don't sit down, baby; we're all on our way out.

GWEN: All the time we were on that fuckin' world cruise, it was just like—not what we'd planned at all. I'll never forgive you for chickening out of that—

KEN: I didn't chicken out.

GWEN: No shit, it was like what the hell are John and me doing in fuckin' Europe, you know? The whole idea was going off to escape from your draft thing—it didn't make any sense.

KEN: Wait a minute. Did I leave you in the lurch?

GWEN: You sure as hell did. John came back, said you weren't going; we cried like babies!

KEN: What did he tell you I said, "Duty calls"? "My country right or wrong"?

GWEN: June's really got your number; you never commit to anything. Holy Christ, smell that air!

KEN: Lavender.

JUNE: Appropriately.

GWEN: Los Angeles smells like a sewer.

JOHN: Let's go celebrate. Come on.

JUNE: You three go on.

KEN: Not tonight. I've got to turn in. I've got to work tomorrow afternoon. I haven't exercised today. Not tonight.

GWEN: This is the last night we're here.

JOHN: I bet that really rips them up.

KEN: No, I'm just beat.

JOHN: Come on, June, let's go.

JUNE: You go on.

JOHN: Come on, babe, I want to show you the night life around here.

KEN: Crickets, frogs, chiggers, owls.

JOHN: You need a sweater, need a coat?

GWEN: No, I'm fine.

JOHN: You're sure, now?

GWEN: I'm sure.

JUNE: We'll see you in the morning.

GWEN: Yeah, see you tomorrow.

JOHN: Hey, Wes, we're gone. (GWEN *and* JOHN *exit.* SALLY *sneaks down the stairs and goes out on the porch*)

WESTON: (*Still on the porch with his guitar*) Hey, what's happening, Sally? I thought you'd gone to bed.

SALLY: I sneaked down. I'm going to the garden.

JUNE: You left them in the lurch. (*Looks at* KEN *for a long moment, then gets up and turns off the light on* KEN*'s desk*)

SALLY: It didn't rain. There's even going to be a moon. (WESTON *stops the guitar*) Look at that sky.

JUNE: I'll see you in the morning. (*She goes upstairs*)

SALLY: You haven't seen anything?

WESTON: Wasn't really lookin'.

SALLY: (*To the sky*) We know you're up there. We won't hurt you. We want to see you.

WESTON: We'd like to talk with you.

SALLY: You can trust us.

WESTON: No shit.

SALLY: Please show yourself to us again. We won't tell a soul!

KEN: (*Gets up. Picks up his crutches*) With the stomach, not the arms. (*Moves to the center of the room*) Cha-cha-cha. (*Painfully gets into a sitting position in the middle of the floor. He stretches out on his back to rest a moment*)

SALLY: (*Pause*) No. Not tonight. (*To* WESTON) Good night. (*To* KEN) Good night, in there.

KEN: (*Who has heard her*) Night, doll; go to bed.

SALLY: (*To the sky*) Good night. (*She goes off into the garden.* KEN *begins to do sit-ups.* WESTON *continues to play.* JED *comes in, changed into his jeans.* KEN *is panting very hard*)

KEN: (*Exhausted*) Oh, God . . . I'm just knocked out. I simply will not be ready for the Winter Olympics this year. I really . . . have done myself . . . in. I cannot teach those kids, Jed . . . We can't stay here . . . I can't walk into a classroom again . . . (JED *picks him up, holding him in his arms. Leaning his head against him*) I really have knocked myself out. (JED *holds him a moment, then carries him upstairs*)

JED: Hang in there.

(WESTON *continues to play for a moment*)

Act II

The porch. JED *is sitting in the sunshine, referring back and forth between two books, trying to compose a letter on a legal-size yellow pad. A bell tolls in the distance, fifteen seconds between each deep, heavy stroke.*

SHIRLEY *enters. She enjoys being alone with* JED *for a moment. She looks out over the garden, quite forgetting that* JED *does not see her there. She notices the bell.*

SHIRLEY: Oh! Listen!

JED: (*Jumps a foot*) Oh, God.

SHIRLEY: "Ask not for whom the bell tolls . . ."

JED: It tolls for Harley Campbell.

SHIRLEY: Who?

JED: Your Aunt Sally went to the funeral. They ring the bell before the service and after the service.

SHIRLEY: Oh. Oh, God, now it sounds horrible. Oh, God, that's mournful.

JED: If the man made more than a hundred thousand a year and left a widow, they ring it all during the service as well.

SHIRLEY: We, of course, are the first. (*He looks at her, not understanding*) To arise this morning.

JED: You're the last.

SHIRLEY: Last?

JED: You're up in time for brunch.

GWEN: (*Inside, on phone*) What the fuck for, dial one?

SHIRLEY: Gwen is up?

JED: Yeah. And on the phone.

SHIRLEY: Uncle Kenny's up?

JED: Yeah, Sally and I had breakfast at seven, I drove her to church, woke up Ken, and we made an herbal anti-fungus concoction guaranteed to fail, and sprayed thirty-five phlox plants. With Wes's, uh . . . supervision.

SHIRLEY: (*Adjusts*) Oh. Yes . . . I slept . . . fitfully. I tossed, I . . .

JED: Turned?

SHIRLEY: I had this really weird dream. I was being chased by a deer. All through the woods, over bridges, this huge deer. What does a dream like that mean?

JED: Did he have antlers?

SHIRLEY: I don't remember. Why? (JED *goes back to his books*)

JED: If you happen to dream about seven fat cows and seven lean cows, I know what that one means.

SHIRLEY: I would never dream of a cow.

JED: Not a feisty young heifer? Jumping fences, trying to get into the corn?

SHIRLEY: Oh, please. I certainly hope you don't think of me like that! I am not a common cow! I am a . . . flower, Jed. Slowly and frighteningly opening her petals onto the spring morning. A trimu-a-timulus, a timu—

JED: What? A mimulus? You're probably a mimulus.

SHIRLEY: What's a mimulus?

JED: Mimulus is a wild flower. Pinkish-yellow, the monkey flower, they call—

SHIRLEY: No, not that one. Not a monkey flower! I am a . . .

JED: What?

SHIRLEY: Well, not—I don't know. And it's important, too. But . . . I can *see* it. A nearly white, small, single . . .

JED: What about an apple blossom? The first tree of spring to—

SHIRLEY: No, oh, God, no. And grow into an apple? A fat, hard, red, bloated, tasteless apple? For some crone to bake in a pie for her ditchdigger husband to eat without even knowing it? Oh, God. Never. I'm more than likely the daughter of an Indian chief. My mother was very broad-minded and very promiscuous.

JED: So I've heard.

SHIRLEY: (*Thinks*) I am a blossom that opens for one day only . . . and I fall. I am not pollinated. It's too early for the bees.

They don't find me. And I fade. Dropping my petals one by
—what kind of flower is that? (*He thinks a moment*) A wild
rose?

JED: No, you wouldn't flower till May at the earliest. There'd
be bees lined up around the block.

SHIRLEY: Well, *what?* God. Daisies are when? (*He shakes his
head*) Peony?

JED: There are some anemones . . . that bloom very early.

SHIRLEY: An anemone . . .

JED: The original ones are from Greece, so they're all claimed
by heroes who fell in battle and their blood seeped into the
ground and anemones sprang up, but I think they've found
one or two somewhere else that haven't been claimed yet. I
have a picture of them somewhere.

SHIRLEY: Could you find it?

JED: It's around; I'll look it up.

SHIRLEY: (*Hand on sleeve*) Jed. Thank you. This is, you know,
very important to me.

JED: (*Mock seriousness*) Shirley. It's important to us all.

SHIRLEY: I know.

JED: We don't dwell on it because we try to spare you the
pressure of all our expectations. We multitudes.

SHIRLEY: I know. But don't. Don't spare me. It makes me
strong.

GWEN: (*Offstage, on phone*) Yeah, well screw you, too. I don't like the way you're handling this whole thing. (*Slams phone down*)

KEN: (*Coming out*) She hasn't been off the phone all morning. Your mother was up at the crack of ten and is making bath buns.

JED: Bath buns?

SHIRLEY: Believe me, you don't want to know. God, when she gets domestic, there's no hope.

KEN: She speaks not with forked tongue.

JED: I'm no good at this; you'd better reconsider.

KEN: No way, do it yourself.

SHIRLEY: What are you doing?

JED: I'm trying to answer a letter.

KEN: I think there's a harpy in the bottom of our garden. (*Yelling*) Yo! Aunt Sally!

SALLY: (*Offstage*) I see you, I see you. Don't rush me.

KEN: She's at the roses again. (*Yells*) Thought you went to Old Man Campbell's funeral.

SALLY: (*Offstage*) Oh, fine. Old Man Campbell. (*Coming in*) Imagine Harley Campbell being Old Man Campbell. I remember when Old Man Campbell was Harley's grandfather. But you're right. There's always an Old Man Campbell.

SHIRLEY: I retired late, of course. I was packing.

JED: Thought you were here for another two weeks.

SHIRLEY: I will probably return after only a few days; I can't imagine Nashville to hold anything of real interest.

KEN: I'm quite sure the city of Nashville is not ready for you.

JUNE: (*Offstage*) Outside, everyone outside. This is just the first batch.

SALLY: (*Arriving at the porch*) No, no, I couldn't do it. That's the hottest place I've ever been in my life.

SHIRLEY: Gird your loins; Mom's making bath buns.

SALLY: Oh, dear. No, the minister is mad at the whole congregation. They voted down a new air-conditioner, so he shut the old one off and told them it broke . . .

JUNE: (*In and out*) This is just the first batch; another coming.

SHIRLEY: Oh, God.

SALLY: He's trying to sweat them out. They'll never give in. A good battle, especially if it's over money, brings out the stoic in them.

KEN: Looks like it's done you in.

SALLY: Oh, I must . . . That's quite a walk. Don't look at me.

KEN: Why didn't you call someone to pick you up?

JED: (*Overlapping*) I could have—

SALLY: (*To* JED) I walked that road to school before even your mother was born.

KEN: You didn't know his mother. She could have been fifty. He might have been the—what's the expression?

JED: Last fruit on the tree.

KEN: I wasn't going to say that.

SALLY: I'm afraid I've thrown a wrench in our scheme.

KEN: Have you two been scheming?

SALLY: What terrible houses they've built along the road. Windows right out to the street. I'd feel naked as a jay. Oh, dear.

KEN: Don't walk that again. There's always someone here to drive you.

SHIRLEY: (*With a letter* JED *has received*) That's very impressive. "Sissinghurst Castle. Property of the National Trust."

JED: Come on.

KEN: The lucky bastards.

SHIRLEY: Have you been there?

JED: Huh? Yeah.

KEN: Before we laid out the garden, we took a tour of the competition.

SHIRLEY: Is it fabulous? (JED *groans*) "Mr. Jed Jenkins, Esquire . . ."

JED: In other words, not Sir or Lord.

SHIRLEY: "First of all, we are writing to confirm the identification of your rediscovery of the Slater's Crimson China rose . . ."

KEN: Thank you so very much, though actually we did know that from the Royal Horticultural Society and Kew Gardens.

SHIRLEY: It's very exciting to have discovered a rose everyone thought was lost ages ago. How did it get here?

KEN: We assume someone planted it.

SHIRLEY: "Which bloomed in our test garden this summer and will be moved to a prominent position in the rose garden this autumn."

KEN: Do you love it? Only the greatest rose garden in the world.

SHIRLEY: How did they get it?

KEN: We sent it to them.

JED: They asked us for it.

SHIRLEY: "And second—" Should that be "second of all"?

KEN: Certainly not. Never. —Though, "which bloomed" could less pretentiously be "that bloomed."

SHIRLEY: "Second we would like to inform you that—"

GWEN: (*Entering, followed by Weston*) Oh, God, would you feel that fuckin' sun? Don't let me fall asleep. I fry like a starfish. (*Flops down in the sun*)

SHIRLEY: "Second we would like to inform you that the Phyle-Hastings Nursery has—"

GWEN: I read that letter and they're so full of it.

SHIRLEY: If you please.

GWEN: Sorry. Hand me a cup.

SHIRLEY: ". . . Nursery has requested the honor of adding this rose to their catalogue so it can once again be propagated and grown as it deserves. You of course will be credited with this important rediscovery . . ."

JED: (*Embarrassed*) Blah, blah, blah, blah.

GWEN: (*Overlapping*) They are so full of it. No way, baby—

SHIRLEY: (*Overlapping*) He rediscovered it, I don't know why not.

GWEN: You check with a lawyer before you sign anything. The limeys would as soon rip you off as look at you.

KEN: They did raise it, after all.

GWEN: Right, and lost it. Fuck 'em. They want it so bad they can pay for it. Not without a commission. Have you got Sweet 'n Low? Oh, forget it.

SHIRLEY: How was the celebration?

GWEN: When?

SHIRLEY: The fireworks you went to last night?

GWEN: Oh, hey, I wanted to come back and get you. It was great. There—

SHIRLEY: They were pretty?

GWEN: —were these really—what? The fireworks? You've never seen anything so lame in your life.

KEN: Present company always excepted.

GWEN: There were these— (*Slaps him*) —field hands—

KEN: (*Overlapping*) You would strike a crippled fairy.

GWEN: These really randy, country Republican high school juniors drinking beer out of a paper sack. You've never seen a hornier collection of male—

SHIRLEY: I would not have been interested.

GWEN: —brawniness in—oh, God, it was John and Kenny when we were in Berkeley. They were exactly the same randy farmhands when we first met. I suddenly understood you completely.

KEN: Me? A farmhand? Son of my father who never farmed a day in his life?

GWEN: It was you, I don't care. They even look like you looked then. They still have long hair.

KEN: John and I moved in quite a different circle from your—

GWEN: I don't care. You're such a snob.

KEN: As the son of the New World mobile-homes dealership for southern Missouri and northern Arkansas—

GWEN: Sure. And Johnny was a dentist's son, I don't care—

KEN: The only dentist in town. We were quite a different social strata from the horny river trash you're trying to associate with us.

GWEN: Horny river trash; that's exactly what they were.

SALLY: Buddy did very well with his mobile homes. But I never liked the house he built in town.

GWEN: I don't care—

KEN: Well, June got a pretty penny for it when she sold it. I think it was a pretty penny, she wouldn't let me see it.

JED: Simple modesty.

KEN: Sibling rivalry. I had first choice.

SALLY: You were right to choose the farm. This has always been the Talley place.

GWEN: I don't care. "You can take the boy off the farm, but you can't—"

KEN: ". . . take the farm off the boy"?

GWEN: You were exactly like that. (*Hits his leg*) Ouch!

KEN: Fiberglass! Light but strong.

GWEN: You both went to the same grubby high school—
you—

KEN: That is a brand-new building, and we went to a different grubby high school—

GWEN: —You can't tell me you didn't drink beer out of a sack. You jerked off behind the same bushes they do.

KEN: I profess to have no memory of the bushes I jerked off behind.

JED: Very fickle.

KEN: Well, I warned you. (JOHN *enters*)

GWEN: Honey, good, tell them. There was one blond stud—
what was his name, you said you knew him.

JOHN: Jim Pendergast's little brother. Only he's assumed a very sinister style.

KEN: Decidedly unstable family.

GWEN: I don't care, he was gorgeous. Shirley would have loved him.

SHIRLEY: I don't think about men physically. I never have. I think about all people spiritually.

GWEN: I know, but you gotta get over that real quick.

SHIRLEY: A sensitive nature is more important to me than—

GWEN: Yeah, but you're right at that age where you can't tell the difference between sensitive and queer as a three-legged ostrich. (*To* JOHN) Oh, baby, at noon our time you gotta call

Schwartzkoff, because they're really screwing up. I don't care if we have to fly back to L.A. tonight, we have to straighten him out.

JOHN: He called here? Why didn't I hear—

GWEN: I called him, 'cause we hadn't heard from him and when he's silent for three days it means he's got something up—

JOHN: Honey, we got a recording session—

GWEN: I don't care. I have to think about one thing at a time. They aren't going to do what we want unless we really lean on him.

JOHN: He just panics. I told you it'll be all right. I'll worry about that. You worry about Nashville.

GWEN: (*Backing down a bit*) No lie, though, he started in on the inner politics of Tasmania and the state wages precedent, and the whole song all over again. He's really not listening to us at all.

JOHN: I know. I'll talk to him. You worry about you.

GWEN: Lean on the son of a bitch. He doesn't have a leg to stand on.

KEN: Begging my pardon. (JUNE *comes in with breakfast: "Here it is"*)

JOHN: (*To* KEN) Hey, your name's going to be mud, too.

KEN: Why's that? Not that I mind. Kenneth Mudd.

JED: Mudd Talley, I think.

GWEN: Oh, yeah, we talked to your boss. What a prick.

JOHN: We talked to Mac. Boy, he never changes.

JUNE: Wouldn't you know he'd be there.

SHIRLEY: Who's Mac?

JUNE: Mac McConnell; principal of the high school.

KEN: Superintendent, now.

JUNE: God, I hated him almost as much as he hated me.

GWEN: No, he said he'd like to see you while you're down.

JUNE: No way.

GWEN: It was John he hated. Said he suspected him of cheating on tests.

JOHN: You believe him still harping on that after ten years?

SHIRLEY: Why is Uncle Ken's name mud?

JOHN: He still thinks you're going to be teaching there this fall.

KEN: He is very mistaken.

JOHN: You ought to call him.

JED: What did you tell him?

JOHN: I'm not going to tell him nothing. Mac thinks you're happy as a pig in shit.

SHIRLEY: Please, I'm trying to eat Mother's cooking.

GWEN: He was very excited about one of his students returning to the fold.

KEN: The prospect excites me not at all.

GWEN: Listen, who can know anything? Last year when we saw you in St. Louis . . .

JED: Two years ago.

GWEN: Was that two years ago? That was all you were talking about. Jed was going to build this garden, you were going to teach.

JOHN: Once again SuperFag's—

KEN: Don't start on that again.

JUNE: Actually, Kenny came down to the school this May and let him little self get frightened away. He visited the classrooms and—

KEN: (*Overlapping*) Yes, Jed and I visited that lovely new building this May, before school let out. Dear old Mac was a little edgy about Jed, he couldn't quite put that together—

JED: I think he was coming pretty close.

KEN: Probably be thrilled. An opportunity to exhibit his liberal tolerance. But other than that, I found him quite pleasantly condescending, didn't you?

JED: No complaints. Said he liked gardens.

KEN: And I had the pleasure of being introduced to the four classes I would be teaching this fall.

JED: Well, actually only three—

KEN: (*Annoyed*) Well, okay, three. I begged off the fourth and went back to the car.

JED: Went in full of piss and vinegar, came out white as a sheet.

KEN: I just wasn't quite ready for them; or they certainly weren't ready for me. We don't have any milk out here, I can't drink—

GWEN: What did they do?

JED: He just overreacted.

KEN: (*Overreacting*) I certainly did not overreact! June, could you hand me my—crutches.

JUNE: (*Overlapping*) No one had prepared them for him— Mac has always been about as tactful—

KEN: (*Biting*) No, I think it was more a question of a sincere lack of rapport.

GWEN: A lot of messy questions, right?

KEN: No, I was quite prepared for the messy questions. Dry urbanity; humorous self-deprecation.

JED: The kids wouldn't look at him. (*Pause. Nobody looks up*)

KEN: Which God knows I should have been prepared for, but for some reason I was not.

JOHN: They were grossed out, for God's sake.

KEN: Well, if I had some deep-seated need to teach, trying to get at Johnny Young's speech problems will fulfill that quite nicely for a few more weeks.

GWEN: That's all too fuckin' humanitarian; I never trust that gig—it's creepy.

KEN: Not at all, the gimp leading the gimp; we form a very cozy symposium.

JOHN: So, do both.

JUNE: Came running back to St. Louis hot to sell the house and hit the road.

KEN: Hardly running.

GWEN: Well, listen, more luck to me. When can you leave?

KEN: Drop a hat!

WESTON: (*After a pause*) Out of a paper sack?

GWEN: Yeah, passing these quart beer bottles in paper sacks. All very covert. None of them over seventeen. Strictly from twenty-four-hour hard-ons.

JOHN: The lucky stiffs.

KEN: Lucky now to get it up in twenty-four hours. Knock on wood. (*Hits a spoon on his leg*)

WESTON: Knock on wood? Knock on wood?

GWEN: I thought you said they were fiberglass.

KEN: A technicality.

WESTON: Oh, shit.

SHIRLEY: If you please.

GWEN: Oh, you're too much. We told you Kenny had wooden legs from his Vietnam—

KEN: "Tour," we call it.

WESTON: Oh, wow.

KEN: Heavy, huh?

WESTON: Oh, wow. I thought you meant he could drink a lot of sake.

JOHN: That's a hollow leg.

WESTON: No shit. How come?

KEN: Well, it was either accept their kind offer of a prosthetics device or find a position as a very cumbersome basketball.

SHIRLEY: Oh, no.

KEN: And I opted for a semblance of mobility.

JUNE: Unless you could hand-pick both basketball teams.

KEN: No, no, I've never been much attracted to sweaty ectomorphs.

JUNE: I don't know. I always thought of John as a sweaty ectomorph.

KEN: Oh, please. That was many moons ago.

JUNE: Only fifteen years.

SHIRLEY and WESTON: *Only* fifteen years?

JOHN: But those were pretty hot years back in Berkeley.

KEN: One had to move with the times. (JED *goes into the house*)

GWEN: Oh, you were sleeping with June at the same time, it couldn't have been all that hot.

SHIRLEY: *No!* Oh, ugh! How could you. Oh, gwackk! Oh, not *him!*

JUNE: I thought she was talking about me. (*To* SHIRLEY) Oh, shut up; you're too much.

JOHN: Everyone was making it with June.

GWEN: Your mother was a bigger pop-tart than I was.

KEN: Not at all, not till after you moved in and she started running with the—what do you call them?

SALLY: The wrong crowd, I think.

KEN: When we were in school here we used to sleep over and diddle with each other.

JOHN: We were twelve years old.

SALLY: You didn't, either. Here at this house?

KEN: Certainly not, the house in town.

JUNE: Why do you think I sold it?

SALLY: The two of you?

JUNE: The three of us.

SHIRLEY: Oh, that's—

SALLY: It certainly is.

KEN: I'd been in love with you for years.

JOHN: You were not. That was just diddling.

KEN: Oh yeah, remember the double date when you couldn't get Margy Majors to go all the way—

JOHN: One time. And I was drunk.

KEN: Well, I wasn't. I had planned it all week. I knew damn well you weren't going to get anywhere with Margy.

GWEN: Oh, God. Remember going all the way!

KEN: And right after you gave your senior ring to Betty Hernquist I distinctly remember tripping her in the hall.

JOHN: Gave it to her to prove it didn't mean anything to me, then the bitch wouldn't give it back.

KEN: I must have been in love with you at least two years before we ran off to Berkeley. He was never out of this V-neck, light-blue cashmere sweater, full of holes.

JOHN: Mostly from you poking your finger in them.

GWEN: He's ticklish.

JUNE: Very.

KEN: Well, then you discovered the Copper Queen.

GWEN: That would be me.

JUNE: Nobody said John didn't know a good thing when he saw it.

GWEN: Damn straight. (JED *returns with milk and* KEN's *cane*)

KEN: And they all lived happily ever after.

GWEN: Oh, I loved us then. I remember once we bought twenty dollars' worth of daffodils and June and I ran up and down, giving them to all the stalled drivers on the Nimitz Freeway.

WESTON: Why?

GWEN: June had decided they were wonderful.

JUNE: They hated us. The traffic started moving; we nearly got run down.

KEN: You were decidedly before your time.

GWEN: That fuckin' war! Damn, it fucked us. It broke my heart when we weren't together. If you'd come with us to Europe, everything would have been so different. You would never have been in Nam, you wouldn't have been injured; June wouldn't have gotten militant and estranged from us.

WESTON: I read this book. Like about war experiences in Nam? It said shock and dope were like common. In the goddamned reading room; Fairleigh Dickinson University.

KEN: I defy anyone to diagram that sentence.

WESTON: Really heavy.

KEN: The reading room at Fairleigh Dickinson was heavy? Vietnam was heavy or the book was heavy?

WESTON: You were there, man, I can't tell you.

KEN: Nothing was common except the American troops, and we were very common indeed.

WESTON: Like you're trying to be cool, but you still carry it around.

KEN: However awkwardly.

SALLY: Your mother was very proud that you went. I could have killed her.

KEN: Wasn't that interesting? I thought so, too. And ashamed that I came back.

SALLY: Oh, that isn't true.

JUNE: The hell it ain't.

WESTON: You still think about it.

KEN: I don't wake up screaming any more from visions of my buddies floating through the blue sky in pieces, if that's what you mean . . .

WESTON: Oh, shit.

KEN: Exactly that. The dream is more likely of some goddamned general moving down the row of beds in the hospital, handing out medals like aspirin. That's the first thing I saw when I regained consciousness.

JUNE: Desperately looking for heroes.

KEN: Beating the bushes. They found a few, heroic actions in the face of fire.

WESTON: Yeah?

SHIRLEY: Uncle Ken has five medals.

KEN: You may not be proud of that.

WESTON: What was the saving grace?

KEN: Beg pardon?

WESTON: You said a heroic action had to have a saving grace.

KEN: Silliest thing I ever heard of—

WESTON: Like with the Eskimo, you said there was no saving grace in—

KEN: Oh, Weston, doll, I'm all in favor of your Eskimo hero. I think he was a man among men. I completely blame the family. You see, if you had said that the warrior farted on the walrus blubber—

WESTON: —caribou meat—

KEN: Be that as it may, and it stank so badly that the family could hardly eat it, but they managed and survived, we could perhaps accept that as an unpleasant but not altogether vainglorious moment in the history of the Eskimo. I thought at the time that the family was too picayune for a myth.

WESTON: Oh.

KEN: See?

WESTON: Yeah.

KEN: Yeah. The family disappointed me deeply.

WESTON: So the saving grace—

KEN: —would have been surviving. Don't choke on it, don't turn up your nose, swallow it and live, baby.

WESTON: Even if it stinks, man.

KEN: Dig it.

WESTON: Right on.

KEN: They could have forever after been known as the family who bravely ate the fart-thawed meat and went on to become . . .

SALLY: —vegetarians.

JOHN: Baby, we gotta pack if we're going to hit the road by three this afternoon.

JUNE: That'll get you there by when?

JOHN: Five. We're driving to Springfield, hopping a plane.

JUNE: Oh, of course you are. (JED *begins to sing: "Hit the road, Jack, and don't you come back no more, no more, no more, no more. Hit the road, Jack; and don't you come back no more"*)

SHIRLEY: I probably won't stay with you more than a few days; I can just crowd you in as it is.

GWEN: We go everywhere with an open-return ticket.

JUNE: This one is returning before she leaves.

SHIRLEY: There's nothing pressing this week.

JUNE: Can it.

SHIRLEY: What do you mean, can it?

GWEN: I thought you'd decided to let her come.

JUNE: The farthest thing from my mind. I wouldn't consider it.

GWEN: We'll take good care of her.

JUNE: No, not this time; another time.

SHIRLEY: What do you mean? You can't! When have I ever had the opportunity to go some place? This could be the beginning of a whole new horizon for me.

JUNE: Just cool it, because you're not going. The one thing I can't bring myself to do is discipline the brat. I hated Mom for that.

SHIRLEY: Well, you had a good reason!

JUNE: We'll discuss it some other time.

SHIRLEY: We won't discuss it at all! (*Storming out*) I am twenty-one years old and I can do what I want to do!

WESTON: Am I going to have time to help with the cinders?

KEN: Sure.

JOHN: The what?

WESTON: Cinders. They got a problem in their garden. I'm gonna help them out.

JOHN: Yeah? Well, sorry, Jed, there goes Les Tuileries. With Wes loose in the garden, that ought to do it . . .

WESTON: I helped them spray the—what was it?

JED: Phlox.

WESTON: The phlox for mold—

JED: Mildew.

WESTON: —for mildew this morning. This afternoon we got to get over to the school where Talley is going to teach . . .

KEN: . . . is not going to teach.

WESTON: —yeah, and get a load of cinders, and spread them around the—what was it?

JED: Penstemon.

WESTON: Gonna spread them around the penstemon, so the —what was it?

JED: Slugs.

WESTON: —so the slugs can't get at them. See, they got these soft vulnerable bellies—

JOHN: The penstemon?

WESTON: No, the—

JED: (*To* WESTON) Slugs.

WESTON: The slugs. They don't like to crawl over the cinders. You spread the cinders around the plant, it keeps them off it.

JOHN: That's . . . ingenious.

WESTON: Yeah, well, you can laugh, but I saw the damage they done just last night. When it's wet like it's been here, the—

JOHN: Slugs?

WESTON: —the slugs become this major problem. And see, we got to get it done before tonight, see, because they come out as soon as it gets dark. They don't like the light, see.

JOHN: Really.

WESTON: Sure.

JOHN: Why don't you put a light in the garden?

JED: Then the eggplant wouldn't set flower. It requires a period of six hours unbroken dark to set—

JOHN: Jed, you're going to tell me about photosynthesis. I don't want to know about photosynthesis.

JED: Photoperiod.

JUNE: Oh, God . . .

JOHN: What?

JUNE: I was just imagining having a vulnerable belly, crawling over cinders.

WESTON: No, see, you can't think like that.

GWEN: Fuck it, kill 'em. They're ruining the garden.

WESTON: Right, you gotta be like cold-blooded and ruthless. Otherwise, you won't have any—what is it?

GWEN and JUNE and JOHN: Penstemon.

WESTON: Otherwise, you won't have any penstemon. They're really voracious. They eat six times their weight every night. I was reading one of Jed's books.

KEN: I wonder what a slug weighs.

WESTON: It didn't say.

KEN: Oh, well . . .

WESTON: We could catch one and weigh it.

KEN: Does anyone have something I could open a vein with?

WESTON: You know what they're trying to make here? What's the name of that garden in England? The one we didn't see.

JOHN: We didn't see any of them.

WESTON: The one we could have seen, though.

JOHN: I don't remember.

WESTON: Well, that's the one they're trying to make here.

SHIRLEY: (*Who has been standing in doorway*) Sissinghurst Castle Gardens. They're a property of the National Trust.

WESTON: Isn't that far out?

GWEN: You know what would be even better? Just let it all go wild. Let whatever happens to grow all go wild.

JED: That would be one answer. (*The phone rings inside*)

GWEN: Oh, shit. That's Schwartzkoff calling back because I hung up on him.

KEN: It isn't long-distance.

GWEN: Yes, it will be. John, you talk to him. He just keeps saying the same thing to me.

KEN: It isn't long—

JOHN: Honey, you don't hang up on someone who's calling from the Coast— (*He goes*)

GWEN: (*Yelling*) I don't care. He was calling me capricious. I felt like showing him what capricious was. (*To them*) I will never be able to understand why I can't do what I please with my own company. It's like zero percent of the whole—conglomerate.

SHIRLEY: Which one is that?

GWEN: Most of the like branches I own like nothing. Like six percent or fifteen percent. But Helena Copper is one hundred percent mine. Mom left it to me, damnit. I was up there. Oh, God, they loved me. I made a speech, they just went crazy. I told them what I wanted to do, no shit, they carried me around the meeting hall over their heads, like a fuckin' astronaut. I judged a beauty contest. I gave the crown to the plainest girl there. You should have seen her. And she just—bloomed! I'll bet her breasts raised four inches. All you guys—you are such pigs! Who said that? Men are pigs.

SHIRLEY: Rita Hayworth, Miss Sadie Thompson.

GWEN: No, it was—

JUNE: Trust her. Believe me.

GWEN: Anyway, you really are just pigs. The guys started rubbing up against her. She was probably the only virgin to win a beauty contest in the history of the country.

KEN: What did you promise them?

GWEN: Oh, well, see, like I got all this money, but like the Surrogate won't let me raise the— (JOHN *is back, listening in the doorway*) —salaries because of the labor situation in the state—

JOHN: In the industry.

GWEN: Is it the industry? Anyway, like, you remember when we read Marx? What pissed Marx off was the owners making money off the workers, just because the owners own the factory.

JUNE: Exploitation of, yes—

GWEN: I may have failed economic philosophy, but I got that. Well, so I said I'd give them a bonus after the year of all the profit except one percent for me. To make me feel like a capitalist. But they had to divide it evenly, file clerks get as much as managers. They flipped.

JUNE: I'll bet.

GWEN: Only Schwartzkoff is trying to take the profit from Helena Copper and pay for capital improvement in the other branches and claim there aren't any profits this year.

JUNE: And that surprises you?

JOHN: A hair illegal, but done all the time.

GWEN: Well, that really pisses me 'cause those people were great to us. They gave us a picnic. We had pigs' feet. Wasn't it pigs' feet, John?

JOHN: It certainly tasted like pigs' feet to me. Oh, shit. The phone's for Ken or June, either one.

JUNE: I'll get it.

JOHN: Sorry. (*Drifts back with her*) We going swimming later?

JUNE: I can answer the phone by myself.

JOHN: We've hardly talked this whole visit.

JUNE: That really rips me up. (*She is gone*)

GWEN: How did you know that wasn't Los Angeles? You couldn't possibly know that just from the ring.

KEN: My affliction has given me great powers to see into the future.

WESTON: Far out.

KEN: Far, far out into the future, Wes. My father was a lowly Ozark trailer dealer, but my mither beyonged to ya yipsies. (*With a Hungarian accent*) Let me see your hand. You have a very long lifeline. You don't have to worry about cancer or heart trouble. You die of old age. You not be much sick. You healthy, only— (*His reading runs without stop; the others run along with it*)

WESTON: Don't dump anything heavy on me.

GWEN: You gotta hear it so you know how to deal with it.

SHIRLEY: No, I never want to know a thing.

GWEN: It gives you strength.

KEN: —you don't take care of yourself the way you should. You all the time too busy to take care of youself. You got much success—very interesting hand.

WESTON: That callus is from the guitar.

KEN: That shows you very musical. You got much success but people try to bring you all the time down. Some people pretend to be you friend, but no you friend. They want bad things should happen to you. One person or more person want you not to be happy. You are not so happy as you should be because of these people. These people bring you down. They tell you things they don't believe; want you do things they no believe.

WESTON: That's enough. Thank you. That's good. (*He cannot get his hand from* KEN)

KEN: (*Without stopping*) They want you not be happy. They doing terrible things; get in you way. I am spiritual woman, I going to help you. I light candle for you. I spiritual person, you need somebody light candle for you. These people—

WESTON: You're really good. That's fine. Come on. Make him quit.

KEN: (*Continuing*) —stand in you way, try to knock you down. Wish you bad. Do such bad things. We do something for each other. You give me five dollars for the candle, I'm—

WESTON: Oh, no. No. What if I don't have five dollars? What happens if you don't light a candle?—

KEN: (*Overlapping*) —going to think about those people try to stand in you way and lie to you and tell you things not right. I going to light a candle, make those bad people go away. I have to get me coffee. I have to get me something to eat. We help each other. You give me money, how much you got; you give me what you can. I light candle, make the bad go away—

WESTON: Oh, God. (*With wallet*) Gwen, lend me five.

GWEN: Bug off.

WESTON: I don't have a five. What if I don't have it, man, come on . . . Oh, God, they always do this to me. (KEN *takes $10 from the wallet*)

KEN: (*Continuing*) These bad people won't have no power over you if I light a candle 'cause I'm a spiritual woman and you help me I do this for you. You bad need help from these people. (*Pockets money*) Now when can you see me again?

WESTON: Oh, God, they do it every time.

KEN: I want to light a candle. I want to tell you how these bad things can be made go way. You come back tomorrow, I make you feel better.

WESTON: (*Running out*) They do that to me every time. It always gets heavy, they tell you it won't—

JUNE: (WESTON *has run right into her in the doorway*) Hold it a second. Wes, excuse me.

JED: That'll pay for the penstemon seed.

KEN: Every little bit helps. If you'd let me go back out onto the streets. (*Pause*)

JUNE: (*Alarmed but very firm*) Aunt Sally.

SALLY: He went away. I didn't know where he had gone. I got tired of waiting for him.

JUNE: He was very upset when I told him you were here. He said for you to lie down. He'll get here when he can.

SALLY: There is no reason for him to come here. And I'm fine where I am.

JUNE: (*Pause. To them*) She passed out in church. They took her to Dr. Anderson's across the street and she sneaked out on him.

SALLY: I did not. He always tries to take care of more than he can; giving everyone five minutes. I waited as long—

JUNE: Would you please. He doesn't know. He hardly had time to examine her; she may have had a mild stroke, it might just be—

SHIRLEY: What?

SALLY: It was nothing of the kind! I merely blacked out. I do it all the time.

JUNE: When? When have you passed out before? Recently?

SALLY: When I was eleven.

JUNE: You should rest, inside. You can't tell the damage, if it was a stroke, until she's been looked at.

SHIRLEY: (*Overlapping*) Where's the doctor? Why didn't he come here?

JUNE: He'll be here as soon as he's free.

SHIRLEY: Free?

GWEN: You don't tell someone they have had a stroke. You say they've had a slight cerebral disturbance.

SHIRLEY: That sounds better?

GWEN: Daddy lapped it up. If they'd told him he had had a stroke, he would never have recovered.

JOHN: He didn't recover.

SALLY: It was very silly, very embarrassing. And when I woke up, I felt perfectly fine.

KEN: Don't talk. It's cooler out here. She's out of the sun.

JUNE: I don't know if she should be alone or lie down or—

SALLY: —I was sitting there listening to that stupid, vindictive Reverend Poole, and I looked over at that smug wife of his, always looking so pleased to have an occasion to show how easily she can cry. She was like that in school. You'd say, Francine, cry! And she'd burst into tears for you. And I looked at her and there were two of her. Sitting side by side. I just thought, Oh, my God, no. If there's one thing that Lebanon does not need it's another Francine Poole. And I was rubbing my eyes, trying to make one of her go away. Or both of her if possible. And I noticed that there were two Reverend Pooles giving that vacuous eulogy, and two pulpits and two caskets and it was just all too—much. And I got up to get the—hell out of there before there was two of me, and—

JUNE: And passed out in the aisle.

SALLY: Everyone must have enjoyed that. I woke up in Dr. Anderson's office, with him clucking at me, and I felt very rested. But there was only one of him. Wouldn't you know.

JED: Too bad. Town could use another Dr. Anderson.

KEN: Where's Dr. Cranefield?

JED: On vacation. Anderson's overloaded.

SALLY: Well, I wasn't going to wait all day for the man to tell me to go home. I wanted a glass of water, I still haven't had one.

GWEN: Double vision is one of the symptoms of a—slight cerebral disturbance.

SALLY: I realized that while I was walking home. I had nurse's training during the war—

JUNE: Walked? You walked here from town?

SALLY: I didn't get in the least tired. No one has ever paid the slightest attention to me, so please don't now. I don't know how to cope with it. I'm sixty-five years old and I have a perfect right to have a stroke. I've suffered a trauma.

JUNE: You rest after something like that. You don't go for a five-mile hike.

SALLY: I came home slowly. It is only a mile and a half. I didn't go jogging.

JUNE: She's too much. I'm arguing with her. I'm killing her. (SHIRLEY *brings* SALLY *a glass of water.* SALLY *takes a sip, and puts the flower she carries in the glass*)

KEN: You really are too much.

SALLY: Please stop looking at me like someone has dumped a dead elephant on your porch.

GWEN: You know, she's right. It's not all that serious. Really, you should listen to me. I mean, between me and Dad, I've spent more time in the hospital than most nurses. Where's John? (JOHN *has left the porch*)

SHIRLEY: He's on the phone.

SALLY: Oh, dear, everyone is going to call. You must tell people I can't be disturbed or all those hypocrites are going to line up outside the door all day tomorrow.

KEN: We'll tell them you're in a coma. (WESTON *drifts back in*)

SALLY: What a scandal to have ruined Harley's funeral. I looked for where he carved his initials on the pew, but I couldn't find them. Certainly the only mark he ever made on anything.

KEN: Would you please not talk. What do you do with her?

SALLY: Pinched me on the fanny and his wife knew it, too. Good Lord, she married him for that huge old house, now she's too old to enjoy it. Must be seventy. She came here from Rogersville. Tried to take over the town. They still call her the Foreigner. God knows what they call me. Jezebel, I'd think. Married a Jew, thrown out of my family—

KEN: Not Jezebel. Naomi, maybe.

JUNE: You were not thrown out of the family.

SALLY: I was! I was thrown out of the family. Had to leave town. Your father said Matt was a no-good Jew and was only interested in the farm. He never forgave Matt for making more money than he did with his trailers.

KEN: Aunt Sally, please don't talk.

SALLY: Well, darling, with you all acting like everything I say might be the last word I utter, I want to be sure I get it all in.

JUNE: Sally, I absolutely forbid you to enjoy this.

GWEN: What's the point if you don't get off on it?

SALLY: Pino's made Harley look very waxy.

JUNE: Who did what?

SALLY: I said Pino's Funeral Home. They made Harley look very waxy.

KEN: A decided improvement, I'd think.

SALLY: Oh, he looked marvelous, but he didn't look like Harley. He always had such dry skin. They should have powdered him. I nearly did it myself. You remember Mrs. Farthing?

JUNE: No.

KEN: Taught algebra.

JUNE: She couldn't possibly still be alive.

SALLY: Oh, yes. She looked at poor waxy Harley and said she supposed death was something we none of us could avoid. But she looked like she thought she might have an angle.

JUNE: How can you tell? Fool that I am, I keep listening to see if you sound normal. You've never sounded normal in your life.

SALLY: Well, don't listen to me. And don't look at me as if it were only a matter of time. It's always only a matter of time.

JUNE: No one said anything about—

SALLY: I refuse to talk about dying.

KEN: How do you get the woman to shut up?

SALLY: I never met anyone who knew the least thing about it. Start talking about death, you end up talking about life, and a good thing, too. (JOHN *comes back out*)

JUNE: Dr. Anderson said she left a candy box in his office.

KEN: Oh, God.

SALLY: I've always had the feeling death wasn't all it was cracked up to be.

KEN: You left Uncle Matt in the office?

SALLY: What are you talking about?

JUNE: The candy box.

SALLY: Well, that's as good a place for it as anywhere. Tell him to keep it. Who needs it.

JUNE: If he brings it back, I'll kill him.

SALLY: That's all taken care of. (*To* WESTON) Matt didn't believe in death and I don't either . . .

KEN: I beg your pardon?

SALLY: There's no such thing. It goes on and then it stops. You can't worry about the stopping, you have to worry about the going on. Is that a hummingbird? Is that a bat?

JED: Where?

SALLY: No. Gone.

JED: There's a family of hummingbirds. We see the daddy a lot.

KEN: How is "that" all taken care of?

SALLY: That is taken care of privately. (*Pause. Phone rings offstage*)

KEN: That one is long-distance.

JOHN: I'll get it. (*Exits*)

GWEN: How do you know that?

KEN: (*To* WESTON) Let me see your hand. Oh, you have very good lifeline—

WESTON: No, no, no, no . . .

GWEN: This place is heaven. I don't want to go to Nashville at all, man. I get more tense every minute.

WESTON: That won't happen again.

GWEN: No shit. Feel my back.

KEN: That won't happen; you'll relax, you'll feel fine.

GWEN: I just feel the tension creeping up my arms right to my jaws. My hands are like ice. Kenny, when could you be out, you know?

KEN: What, love?

GWEN: Like, if I'm gonna freak out till I have my own studio. Like, we could cancel this gig in Nashville, go back to L.A., and see what's eatin' Schwartzkoff while they're fixing up a place for us here and come back in August. What's it gonna cost me?

KEN: I've never built a recording studio, I really wouldn't—

GWEN: No, man, the place. What are you asking for it? You got nineteen acres, you got the river, what's your price? I mean, I don't do it, the company does it, but I should know what you're soaking us for.

JUNE: There you go, a live buyer.

KEN: It's very weird, selling something to a friend. We have an asking price we haven't come down from, because I'd like to get—

GWEN: Right, sure, top dollar. Listen, I don't bargain. So you're rippin' me off, like that's so new to me? What are you waiting for, some Arab to buy up the whole state? Copper money is as good as oil money, Daddy used to say that—only he was talking about Rockefeller.

KEN: I don't think we can leave quite as fast as you'd—

GWEN: I gotta find a place, Kenny; I can't fart around.

JOHN: (*Entering*) Hey, baby, you're going to have to talk to King, he won't tell me what's up.

GWEN: That's King? Calling here? What does he want?

JOHN: Some deal, some record company; the man's delirious.

GWEN: What record company—

JOHN: He won't tell me, he wants to talk to you. He's got someone lined up to be at the session. Talk!

GWEN: Did you call Schwartzkoff?

JOHN: He wasn't in. Take the call; he's a busy man.

GWEN: Oh, God, I'm going to look peachy with some record company in the studio, my shrink trying to pry open my mouth with his fingers.

JOHN: Would you take the goddamned call. Come on, Wes, move your butt.

SHIRLEY: I want to hear your songs before you leave. Apparently I won't be afforded the opportunity to—

GWEN: Listen, sure, anything you want. Come on, I'm serious about this house. You talk it over. And like August, September.

JOHN: I know, we will. (WESTON *goes inside*)

GWEN: No shit, it's what we been looking for . . . Get a price. And find out when they can be out.

JOHN: I know, we will. (GWEN *is gone*) Uh . . . I been setting up this thing with Jimmy King for three months; suddenly he won't talk . . .

KEN: Yeah . . . frustrating.

JOHN: About your place, Gwen's really got a hair up her butt.

SHIRLEY: Oh, dear.

JOHN: You tell her what you're asking?

KEN: No, we were just getting to it . . . I, uh . . .

JOHN: So what's the bite? Come on, you said you want to travel. What's the price?

JUNE: A hundred seventy-five.

JOHN: Jesus H. You don't want much. We'll give you a hundred and a quarter.

SALLY: For the Talley place? You're joking.

JOHN: What's left of it. Don't kid yourself, you're not gonna get a better offer, you realize that.

KEN: Jack, the thing is . . .

JOHN: Listen, for all we care, you can live here. We wouldn't be here more than five months. Less. What more could you want? Jed can build his goddamned English garden.

KEN: No, come on. The idea was to travel. After we sell the place I never want to see it again. (*Pause*) Jed? (*Long pause*) You're really puttin' me on the spot here. We have over a hundred lilies Jed grew from seed two years ago, going to bloom this August— Gwen wants the place—

JOHN: Oh, piss, Talley, you want to dick around or you want to sell the place? Huh? So? So? So?

KEN: Come on, let up. Jesus.

JOHN: A hundred and a quarter, flat out. What's the problem?

KEN: Boy, you really wheel and deal, here. I didn't expect to have to bargain. God, I hate being such a Froot Loop, but—

SHIRLEY: Take it!

WESTON: (*In and out for his guitar*) It ain't I don't trust you, it's just me, you know? Very big news.

KEN: Gwen wants the place right away—we couldn't—

JOHN: Don't listen to her, stay till Christmas, see your damn lilies—

KEN: You don't even like the place— Gwen wants to grow weeds—

JOHN: I love it, I always have.

KEN: Yeah, but what do you care where you are, as long as there's a telephone.

JOHN: As it happens, Gwen is the one who decides. Whatever she says is fine by me. Whatever makes her happy.

JED: I'm hip.

KEN: But, Jesus, John, the money you spend doing it . . . I mean I know you're trying to gain the whole world, but what are you losing doing it?

JOHN: Everything gets written off. We wouldn't own it. The company would own it. We don't own anything. The company has it all.

JUNE: So she said.

KEN: Come on, we're not blind. How can you buy? What are you buying, the whole record company now? How can you buy a—

JOHN: Oh, for God's sake. Who's doing that? She wants a chance to see if she's any good.

KEN: But how can a person buy something like that just to keep her out of the board meetings of—

JOHN: Oh, fuck, Talley. Stop being such a faggot. Look around you, wake up, for God's sake. You can buy anything!

SALLY: Not for a hundred and a quarter you can't.

JOHN: Okay, that was the wrong thing to say. Listen, I'm just trying to make her happy.

JUNE: Sure, but for whom? The board of directors?

KEN: The Surrogate.

JED: Schwartzkoff!

JOHN: Yeah, see, that's not your business.

KEN: I can't sell for that price. It—

JOHN: You can't sell to me for that price or you can't sell to anybody for that price? I'm not deaf to these insinuations and innuendos that have been floating around. (*Pause*)

KEN: (*Level*) I was very angry when you took off for Europe without telling me, but that's long past.

JOHN: Don't dump that on me.

KEN: The three of us plan for six months to go together, suddenly you two leave a week ahead of schedule, what the hell would you call it?

JOHN: No, I won't take that. You can't lay your goddamned fecklessness on me— I'm not responsible for anything that happened to you in—

KEN: Okay, forget it. Everyone loves you, everyone forgets everything. Nobody's dumping anything on you.

JOHN: What would you call it? No. I did not want you to come. I wanted me and Gwen to get out of the whole steamy situation with both of you.

KEN: Until last night when Gwen said I left you in the lurch, I thought it had been her idea. So you told her I changed my mind. Okay.

JOHN: Yeah. And we had a good cry and left in two days and how long did you stay in Oakland before you actually got called up? One month? Two months?

JUNE: Closer to three.

JOHN: So you're blaming me? I thought you'd fag out. Why did you go, anyway? Did it have anything to do with Gwen and me?

KEN: No.

JOHN: Now I hope everyone heard that.

JED: That's enough.

JUNE: It was just easier to let them take you.

KEN: I have never known why I went, and the question has crossed my—

JUNE: You sure as shit didn't believe in it.

KEN: I sure told myself I didn't.

JUNE: You sat on your damn butt and let them take you because it was fuckin' easier than making a commitment; you fuckin' let them make your commitment for you.

JOHN: Hey, baby, I'll tell you something. The first thing you learn in business is to talk about one deal at a time. Kenneth got us down here because he said he wanted to sell the place. Now, I'll give you a hundred thirty, that's as high as I go.

SALLY: A hundred thirty-five.

JOHN: You bidding against me or are you trying to up the price?

SALLY: I'm bidding against you.

JOHN: A hundred forty.

SALLY: A hundred forty-five.

JOHN: A hundred fifty.

SALLY: A hundred fifty-five.

KEN: Aunt Sally, what the hell are you doing?

JED: I promised her we wouldn't sell the house.

SALLY: Jed said you weren't going to sell the place and we scattered Matt all over the rose garden early this morning. It didn't take ten minutes. And we're not going to sell the place for a hundred fifty thousand. I'm prepared to go to two hundred twenty-six thousand. Kenny, you can sell it to me if you've got to sell.

KEN: Jed? Why did . . . I can't stay here. I am terrified of—

JOHN: Well then, what the fuck did we come up here for? I came here for two reasons: to buy the house because Gwen said you needed money and to talk to June.

JUNE: About what?

JOHN: Could we walk down away from here a minute?

JUNE: I don't think so.

JOHN: Then could Shirley go inside for a while?

SHIRLEY: Certainly not.

JUNE: I don't think you want to go into that right now.

JOHN: I don't have to enumerate the advantages for the kid.

JUNE: Advantages? What the fuck are—

JOHN: Gwen and I both love her. I don't want to seem cavalier—

KEN: Of course not.

JOHN: Just look at the situation. What she is and what we could offer her.

JUNE: And what she could become.

JOHN: Not permanently, just half the year. Just a few months a year—

JUNE: You're out of your mind. You have the balls. You have the balls—

JOHN: Come on, I don't want Gwen to hear this, and I don't think you want Shirley to—

SALLY: I knew goddamned well he didn't want the house. No, young man.

JUNE: I don't give a shit who hears it. Out. You better leave now, and you better never—never mention Shirley again.

KEN: (*Standing*) You better watch what you say, buddy; you're leaving yourself open for one hell of a non-support suit—

JOHN: I have said nothing. I claim no responsibility.

JUNE: Some things you cannot buy, baby! Now leave.

JOHN: All right, forget it; can it. You just by God remember you had the chance.

SHIRLEY: I will live in St. Louis with my mother.

JOHN: Fine, baby, it serves you right. (*Yelling*) Baby, we're leaving here. (*Pushes* KEN *out of his way.* KEN *goes down flat on his back*) Oh, Jesus God. I forgot. I'm sorry, baby, I'm sorry, I forgot completely.

JED: Go on. Don't touch him. Leave. Move. (*He grabs a pair of pruning shears; threatening*)

KEN: I'm not hurt! I'm not hurt! It's okay, Jed.

JOHN: I swear to God, I barely touched you!

JED: (*Overlapping*) You go in to Gwen; I'll get him up.

KEN: I'm okay. (*Still on floor*)

GWEN: (*Bursting into the porch*) Holy shit, they want me! They want me! We're in! Oh, sweet Jesus! Columbia bought our tape! They're releasing the fucker in two weeks! Holy shit, they flipped out! The man is talking like retainers of five thousand a month for the first six months, then renegotiate. The man is talking like we're fuckin' stars.

WESTON: (*Overlapping*) No shit, he's like sellin' it to us. We didn't have to say shit.

GWEN: Two weeks! Two weeks! He's going to have the fucking record on the air. On the motherfuckin' airwaves.

WESTON: He wants it orchestrated, though, he wants strings. Whoever heard of fuckin' strings in a—

GWEN: Damn straight. Violins, fuckin' cellos, the works. Lay it on me. Voice of pain! Shitfire. Baby, we gotta pack. Come on, move your ass. (GWEN *goes offstage*)

JOHN: Baby, there's only one plane. We can't leave here till three! (*Pause*) Listen. I'm your friend, if you know it or not. (*Exits*)

WESTON: John's gonna shit. This cat is a different cat from the one John set up for us. Columbia outbid the cat John bought. She's really good. John don't know.

JOHN: (*Offstage*) Wes, move your tail.

WESTON: I got to go pack. (*Runs to the door. Stops. Politely*) It was very nice meeting you. (*Exits*)

KEN: (*As* JED *starts to pick him up*) Hold it a second. (*A very long pause;* KEN *is nearly crying.* JED *sits beside him, holding his hand*) Jesus. That scares me. (*Fighting tears*) Falling backwards is the one thing the guys always—sometimes I think I'll never dance *Swan Lake* again. (JED *rises and helps* KEN *to stand*)

JUNE: You're quicker than you look.

SALLY: I've never been so scared in my life. And I'm sixty-seven years old.

JUNE: I thought you were sixty-five.

SALLY: I've lied about that since I was twenty.

KEN: I haven't worked out a syllabus.

JED: Yeah, you've got a lot of work to do.

JUNE: Where is that damned doctor?

KEN: I'd better call the Youngs. Tell them I can't see Johnny this afternoon.

JUNE: You go on. I'll take care of Sally.

KEN: This guy is really something else.

JUNE: Did you finally understand what he was talking about?

KEN: Oh, sure, just takes listening to a couple of times. He's into the future.

JUNE: Well, why not.

KEN: You'd think he'd tell me something about his past. Johnny's into science—only in a very esoteric way. Sally and Wes wouldn't like it at all, he's very positive and negative and decidedly eccentric. Space travel, teleportation—and it all ends up— (*Turns on cassette player, and reads from his yellow pad at the same time*) "After they had explored all the suns in the universe, and all the planets of all the suns, they realized that there was no other life in the universe, and that they were alone. And they were very happy, because then they knew it was up to them to become all the things they had imagined they would find." (*Turns off the cassette player.* JUNE *picks up tray with the breakfast dishes and goes inside.* WESTON *comes to the stairs, sits down, tuning his guitar*)

SALLY: You know, if I sold that mausoleum in California, I could dump an awful lot of money into this place. I was just thinking out loud.

KEN: I frankly don't think you should be moved from here.

SALLY: I'm much too ill to travel . . .

JED: Oh, that's out of the question.

WESTON: Hey, Sally, I want you to hear this. Shirley!

SALLY: I'm coming!

WESTON: Talley?

KEN: We hear you. (GWEN *joins* WESTON; *he plays the introduction to his song.* JUNE *comes to the door to listen.* SALLY *gets up*) Are you okay?

SALLY: Well, I can walk.

KEN: You're beatin' me. (SALLY *goes in to listen to them.* SHIRLEY *and* KEN *and* JED *sit on the porch.* SHIRLEY *is crying quietly*)

KEN: What's wrong, doll?

SHIRLEY: I don't care. The important thing is to find your vocation and work like hell at it. I don't think heredity has anything to do with anything.

KEN: Certainly not.

SHIRLEY: You do realize, though, the terrible burden.

KEN: How's that?

SHIRLEY: I am the last of the Talleys. And the whole family has just come to nothing at all so far. Fortunately, it's on my shoulders. (*She gets up, with the weight of the burden on her shoulders.* GWEN *and* WESTON *begin to sing*) I won't fail us. (*She goes into the house.* KEN *and* JED *listen a moment*)

KEN: We had to put in all those damn lilies. If they don't bloom, it's your ass. And you and Weston have got to get cinders this afternoon for the penstemon.

JED: Oh, God. And you have to light a candle for him.

KEN: Maybe he'll write us a song. (*He gets up. Sighs. Picks up the portable recorder*) I've got to go talk to Johnny Young about the future. (*They look at each other a moment. The singers continue.* JED *looks out over the garden, still seated.* KEN *begins to work his way toward the door*)

The song continues as the light fades

YOUR LOVING EYES

Words and music © 1979 by John Hogan

An-y-time   (you) want to leave me an-y-time   you want to go

An-y-time   (you) want to leave   (just) let me know

(You're) much too tired for lov-in and it gets too hard   too hard (to)
If you've emptied your pockets by the sunrise of the bad lies only sand in your hand if you

cry   and if it comes as a slight sur-prise

try   you might find someone who you recognize

repeat and fade

I don't want   to lose   your lov-in eyes

Hunger Pains

From Fad Diets to Eating Disorders—
What Every Woman Needs to Know
About Food, Dieting, and
Self-Concept

MARY PIPHER, PH.D.

Adams Publishing
HOLBROOK, MASSACHUSETTS

Published by Adams Media Corporation
260 Center Street, Holbrook, MA 02343

ISBN: 1-55850-532-6

Printed in the United States of America.

J I H G F E D C B A

Library of Congress Cataloging-in-Publication Data
Pipher, Mary Bray.
Hunger pains : from fad diets to eating disorders—what every woman
needs to know about food, dieting, and self-concept /
Mary Pipher. — Rev. ed.
p.   cm.
Includes bibliographical references.
ISBN 1-55850-532-6 (pb.)
1. Eating disorders—Popular works. 2. Body image. 3. Weight loss.
I. Title.
RC552.E18P54   1995
616.85'26—dc20   95-30720
CIP

This publication is designed to provide accurate and authoritative information with
regard to the subject matter covered. It is sold with the understanding that the pub-
lisher is not engaged in rendering legal, accounting, or other professional advice. If
legal advice or other expert assistance is required, the services of a competent professional person should be sought.
— From a *Declaration of Principles* jointly adopted by a Committee of the
American Bar Association and a Committee of Publishers and Associations

This book is available at quantity discounts for bulk purchases.
For information, call 1-800-872-5627.